CONTENTS

Author's Note	v
Foreword	vii
Summer 2018	1
Autumn 2018	37
Winter 2018/19	85
Spring 2019	135
19th May 2019	193
Appendix 1	215
Appendix 2	217
Appendix 3	219
Acknowledgements	223

THE MIGHTY CHERTSEY TOWN

A year in the life of a non-league club that dared to dream

Alice Graysharp
with
Chris Gay

Photography by Andy Pearson
Foreword by Ian Selley

London | New York

Published by Clink Street Publishing 2019

Copyright © 2019

First edition.

The author asserts the moral right under the Copyright, Designs and Patents Act 1988 to be identified as the author of this work.

All rights reserved. No part of this publication may be reproduced, stored in a retrieval system or transmitted, in any form or by any means without the prior consent of the author, nor be otherwise circulated in any form of binding or cover other than that with which it is published and without a similar condition being imposed on the subsequent purchaser.

ISBN: 978-1-913136-60-4

AUTHOR'S NOTE

When some Chertsey Town supporters (you know who you are!) suggested to me towards the end of the 2018-2019 season that I should write a book about Chertsey Town Football Club's extraordinary adventure in both league and Vase, my work commitments, writing, promoting my published novel, family and home commitments and, of course, football all seemed reasonable excuses. But at Chertsey Town's last home game I realised how bereft I was going to be in the close season between the Wembley Final and the pre-season friendlies. "What else is there for me to do in my summer Saturdays and Tuesdays evenings?" I said to Dave Rayner; even so, the task of putting a book together with a 2019 publication date and the consequently early copy deadline date was daunting.

I then realised that at least half, probably more, of the book had already been written by our indefatigable Club Secretary, my co-author Chris Gay, the provider of the programme match reports and quirky Quill Quips spread throughout the season, all a labour of love and dedication which deserve a wider audience in addition to the faithful regular match attenders. And we needed to go no further than the Club's photographer Andy Pearson for photographs.

So I put my head above the parapet and this souvenir of the season book is the result. Like a club sandwich, layered between the match reports are player pen pictures, Quill articles, players' thoughts about juggling work with football, superstitions and highs and lows of the season, supporters' experiences of following The Curfews and snippets about the club's history, its nickname and its home. In the limited time available to meet the publication deadline I apologise to any players and officials for whom time ran out to interview and to any Club officials and supporters who would have also liked to contribute.

This book is offered as a tribute to all who contributed to the Club's success, whether named or not, whether driving forces or more modest passengers. It is also offered as an encouragement to Chertsey Town supporters of the future, and to non-league football fans everywhere, that a dream that you dare to dream really can come true.

Alice Graysharp
August 2019

FOREWORD
BY IAN SELLEY

I have been following Chertsey Town FC's progress from afar as I have been lucky to be friends with members of the management and backroom staff. It meant I got to watch the games when I was back, either at home or away, as I lived in Dubai. I had to stream the FA Vase Final game which was amazing, albeit very frustrating as I wanted to be there soaking up the atmosphere, and the streaming wasn't the best shall we say… I had looked at flying over for 24 hours for the game so I could make it back for the final week of the Arsenal Academy in Dubai, but there were no return flights. I was in awe seeing my small-town club make it to the final in such a big competition. What made it even better for me personally was knowing the club and the people behind it who have made it what it is today. They have done so much to the club that you just could not imagine; from sorting the pitch out, repainting and refurbing the dressing rooms and bar etc. And to do all of this in the first year is short of phenomenal!

Last season (the first full year of the new management), saw players come in from above leagues. They got automatic promotion… it is a dream that most clubs don't reach year after year, but to also win the FA Vase – in Year 1 – is a huge achievement!

Yes, I followed from afar, but it was great to see the whole town get behind them. The supporters followed the club around. They went to both home and away games. All of my friends that live in Chertsey went to the cup final... It was only natural that I felt as though I was missing out. My friends have become season ticket holders and take their young children down to Alwyns Lane on a Saturday. I wanted to do that with my family.

Luckily, though, I managed to be back in the UK for the Black Cherry Fair, so I didn't miss out on the open-top bus tour. I took my family to watch the town erupt in cheers and song, welcoming the players back after the summer. I know from my time at Arsenal, that this is an experience that the players just won't forget. Any of the team that is involved in something like the open-top bus tour of a town will have a memory that will stay with them forever. Being with your teammates, the Chairman and staff, and seeing the town surround the bus is something that you just don't forget. I can remember it well. The excitement and exhilaration that sat in the pit of my stomach when I first saw that crowd appear is unlike anything I had experienced before or since then. Even remembering this now makes the hairs on the back of my neck stand up, now even after all these years... This memory and the emotions surrounding this will live with the players forever.

The whole town turned out and was in huge support of Chertsey Town Football Club. I hope that seeing this drives them on and makes the players want to stay with the club during the tougher times. I loved to see the town get behind the club, but it hasn't always been like this.

When I was playing for Chertsey in the last year of my playing career, we were lucky to get 80-150 people through the gates. Yet last season, when the team started to do well especially in the cup competition, the crowds were getting bigger and bigger. Fast-forward to the semi-final of the cup competition, the ground looked full. Watching from 7,000 miles away, I could feel everyone's excitement – it was all over Facebook, with friends and family taking their children down to support their local club.

If you ask anyone in Chertsey, they say that they have seen a game and/or supported the team in the open-top bus celebration. At the final itself, there were a good few thousand people that travelled – most people paying to travel up by bus together. And as the result went the right way, it made the parties last a long time – they had a fantastic day. My family and I were just as ecstatic, breaking open the champagne on the final whistle while my daughters ran around in front of the TV shouting, "We are the winners!"

I know it won't be that way all this coming season though. Going up a league is going to be a bit harder, but with the players that they have in the squad, they could do well, and dare I say it, keep winning. If they continue winning, performing and getting good results, I can't see any reason why the supporters won't continue to show up to games. And we need this for the club to continue to thrive.

They should be able to push forward. Now they have guys like Dave Rayner and Mark Turner that are willing to give up a lot of their time and finances to bring the better players in. It is a club that has been lying dormant for so many years. When I was there, there was no drive to push the club forward and drive up the leagues.

But push forward they have and the new management has gone about it the right way. They have involved the community and local businesses. They provide discounts for kids and OAPs. They have improved the bar and facilities… it is 100 times better than it was – especially when compared to when I played there, for starters you can now play on the pitch! This would have been a huge investment from the board to ensure that they had brought the pitch up to scratch, and this has filtered through to the other teams. They have a great reputation at that level and players in the league and above will know that they will be able to train on class pitches. The squad knows that they will be looked after. I hope that this attracts other high-class players to the club while retaining the ones they have.

The players and the management of Chertsey Town Football Club have a lot to feel proud about. I have never seen so many young kids with Chertsey town shirts. If they can continue to build the club through the younger age brackets, I know that the club will continue to do very, very well… And I can't wait to watch it all!

Ian Selley
August 2019

We are the Town
The Mighty Chertsey Town
We think you just don't understand
We play in blue and white
We're deadly dynamite
We are the Mighty Chertsey Town

SUMMER 2018

Dave Rayner, retired businessman, former entrepreneur and Director of Football surveyed the football ground around him and saw that it was good. Deep blue paintwork glistened, lush grass gleamed and whitewashed walls bounced back shimmering heat from one of the hottest summers since records began. The contrast with the ground he had returned to only a few months earlier after 22 years' absence was palpable. Gone was the rusting metalwork, wiped clean were the accumulated years of grimy rainwater staining. Already undertaken or nearly finished were new changing rooms, refurbished tea bar and outside toilets, new perimeter fencing, refurbished referee facilities and repainting of the ground.

"Okay, Dave, that's about it for now. Unless you can spot anything else we can fix before kick off."

Approaching from the path in front of the stand and mounting the double terracing steps, Mark Turner, Chertsey Town's Commercial Manager, indicated the tool box and paint pot he carried.

"No, it's all looking good, time for a cold beer."

Dave Rayner was the architect and Mark Turner the powerhouse of Chertsey Town Football Club's regeneration. Little had Mark imagined as a player for Chertsey Town in the 1993-1994 season that he would be back twenty-five years later spearheading the regeneration of a ground to make it fit for the higher levels of non-league football. Mark takes up the story.

"I came back to Chertsey Town in the summer of 2018. I'd become good friends with Dave Rayner since my Chertsey playing days and I got a call from Dave asking me to help him turn the club around. I spent the summer wielding a paintbrush with a team of volunteers. We renovated the ground – there were no hot showers, for example, and no bar. And what we thought to be simple to deal with often turned out to be complicated. Or time-consuming, such as watering the pitch for which we had the one hose whereas some clubs at a similar level such as Hanwell, Horley and Uxbridge have under pitch water sprinklers. I was still doing the finishing touches just before the first game of our new league season."

For the Chertsey Town Football Club's committee gathering in the clubhouse before the game the contrast couldn't have been more marked between the expectations of the new season and the gloom of the previous March when, languishing near the foot of the Combined Counties Premier Division after a series of similarly dismal seasons, the committee found itself faced with a mass departure of their first team manager and almost all the players. Like the proverbial knight on a white charger Dave Rayner had galloped in to the rescue, offering his services to the club, including underwriting the Club's finances for the coming season provided Chertsey meanwhile retained their Combined Counties Premier League status. Dave Rayner "got involved with Chertsey Town FC for a second time in my life because I wanted a challenge in retirement. I watched a few games and Chertsey kept losing and were struggling in every corner so I then offered to come back as Director of Football with a view to carrying on the following season if they stayed up. Unfortunately the manager was not forthcoming with his strategy and plans to deliver what I required to deliver the success, so arrangements were implemented to replace him. I asked Stuart Cash, whose son plays for Nottingham Forest, if he knew anyone he could recommend for the job of manager. I said I could offer a good playing surface and a renovated ground. I was willing to undertake ground improvements to bring Alwyns Lane back to its former standard which would encourage players to join us.

"Dave Anderson was introduced to me and after a few hours discussing the dream I had for 2018-2019 he agreed to come out of retirement, save us from relegation and find the players to buy into our dream, many of whom dropped to Level 5 or came out of retirement.

"Players left too but with help from Kevin Maclaren who joined us we managed to persuade some players to drop a non-league level or two, which was a great achievement. The whole basis was getting quality players to join us to fulfil their dream of playing at Wembley which I had asked Dave Anderson to fulfil for myself and Chertsey. If you can get players on your side, when things go wrong they're fighting for you. With the mostly new squad I expected Chertsey to win all their games."

Dave Anderson is a former Northern Ireland International goalkeeper who later managed Harrow Borough, AFC Wimbledon and Hendon. Retired and enjoying his golf, when he received a call sounding him out about the Chertsey Town job he was flattered but reluctant to return to management, the most stressful and demanding job in football. "I had a call from Stuart Cash asking me to meet Dave Rayner for a chat about his vision and to see if I was interested. I had retired three years earlier after 30 years. My last three seasons were with Harrow Borough where we managed to avoid relegation each season." He met with Dave Rayner in March 2018 and, impressed with Dave Rayner's vision for the club's future, he decided to take the job and set about acquiring a new team for the club's end of 2017-2018 season's ultimately successful relegation battle.

"When I took over the first team at Chertsey Town FC," says Dave Anderson, "all but four of the team left. The best thing about the players leaving was I didn't need to spend precious time giving them a chance. The team's record before I took over pointed strongly to them not being good enough for the level, so in hindsight the fact that they left helped us turn it round quicker. While it was a surprise, nothing shocks me in the world of football. We only had four days to get a team together to play on the Saturday and we managed to add 15 players in that time. The best thing about the situation was that I was able to get in players I knew which gave us a chance to turn it around as Chertsey were facing relegation. It proved to be a rollercoaster ride to get Chertsey onto an even keel but we avoided relegation with some to spare. Steve Hawkins was helpful in finding the players."

Dave Rayner's vision for Chertsey Town was threefold:
– to attain promotion from the Combined Counties Premier League
– to win the FA Vase
– to reach the third round of the FA Cup.

With Chertsey's first friendly of the season coming up and the memory of the final run-in to the previous season in mind, the hope of a return to Chertsey's glory days of the mid-1990s was dangling before the committee's eyes. Chertsey played five friendlies, producing a mixed bag of results.

Saturday 14th July – Friendly   Hanwell Town 1 Chertsey Town 2

Although we started our session of pre-season warm up matches relatively late, we soon got into the groove at Bisham Abbey's National Sports Centre with a 2-1 win over Isthmian League side Hanwell Town. Eighteen players were involved, ten of which had not previously donned a Chertsey shirt.

Hanwell had the upper hand in the initial manoeuvrings and took a sixth minute lead off a free kick delivered from the right flank. The ball was delivered right into our goalmouth where a host of players tried to intervene but it was their Gareth Chendlik who got the contact to head the ball home.

We steadied and had completely stabilised as the second quarter of the game was entered. It was just after the half hour, though, before it paid dividends with a clean-cut equaliser. A cross, launched deep on the left flank by Aaron Morgan was redirected with a stooping header by Dale Binns, to put the game back into equilibrium at half time.

Inevitable changes were made in the second half that broke up the flow for both sides. The bulk of the swaps were done after us Curfews had taken a fortuitous lead when a weak back pass to the Hanwell goalkeeper was intercepted by an alert Connor Harbridge, who had no difficulty in bypassing the hapless 'keeper and walking the ball into the net.

This being Bastille Day, the Hanwell attack must have thought themselves French revolutionaries by laying siege to the Chertsey goal late on, but unlike the fortunes of the royalist cause of that time, us defenders hung on to the end without further incursions.

Dale Binns

Chertsey's first goal of the new season's friendlies came from the head of Dale Binns. Previously retired from football, coming into the 2018-2019 season at 37 he had never expected to find himself again turning out of an away dressing room in the heat of a July's afternoon sun.

At left midfield, Dale has a long list of non-league clubs on his CV. Most of his footballing career was at Hendon with spells also at Wealdstone, Stevenage, Sutton United, Hayes & Yeading and Woking. He joined Chertsey following "a Hendon reunion last summer [2018] in Windsor in which we played a game and then had a good old booze up. To be honest it was more about the booze up than the game, but it just so happens I did rather well, at which point Dave [Anderson] was trying to tempt me out of retirement." Also instrumental in Dale's decision were the new Chertsey Town captain, Kevin Maclaren, Dave Rayner and Gary Anderson, Chertsey's physio.

Dale's career at Hendon under Dave Anderson was not always plain sailing. "When I was playing for Hendon with Dave, at the time we were playing away to Farnborough. Those days there were no satnavs or smart phones. I was with a few of the boys and we were carrying the kit and travelling to the ground. When we got to Farnborough we realised that we went to the wrong Farnborough as there is also a place in Kent called Farnborough. The Manager gave us a good blasting and we had to drive like crazy to get to the correct location, we made it there 20 minutes before kick off!"

Dale's decision to return to football was not lightly made. Working as a Team Manager for Islington Council, while Saturdays were manageable, "as a married man with two young kids, it's been a struggle with the midweek games, as I do the after school/nursery pick ups and sort them out before the Mrs gets home from work. Then it's literally a high five then dashing to football. Thankfully the Gaffer was understanding from the off which is another reason why I decided to give it a go at the start of the season."

Tuesday 17th July – Friendly   Chalfont St Peter 2 Chertsey Town 0
With another combination of players, and on a small arid pitch at Brunel University, we had slightly the better of the first half but were on the wrong end for most of the second. However, we rallied strongly towards the end. The two Chalfont goals came midway through the second period, one from the boot and another the head. This was a real try out that featured a relatively young side.

Travelling to friendly matches pre-season at Chertsey Town's level of non-league football tends to be local, venturing into nearby English counties at best. This has not always been the case and Dave Rayner recollects a friendly played beyond these shores on 7th June 1994.

"We played a friendly against Sociedad Deportiva Compostela in north west Spain. Chertsey had been going to play a friendly there a previous season but Compostela had been involved in play offs so the friendly that time didn't take place. The following year Compostela got promotion to La Liga and the friendly against Chertsey Town went ahead. Chertsey were 3-0 down at half time in front of a huge crowd who were delighted how the match was going. We'd learned that the Compostela fans thought they were playing Chelsea and I'd grown a beard to look like Ken Bates. Chertsey pulled one back in the second half to end the score 3-1. One of the Chertsey Town players gave his shirt away at the end of the match which was not a good thing as we hadn't budgeted to buy new shirts!"

Saturday 21st July – Friendly　　　　Ascot United 0 Chertsey Town 1

A return to a blazing hot Bisham Abbey National Sports Centre for the second successive Saturday set up another one goal victory, this time against Hellenic League side Ascot United. Dave Anderson had yet to field his preferred starting eleven with a mix and match team featuring the established alongside hopefuls for the coming season. The combination worked well on the day.

The exchanges were pretty well even in the first half but we edged the second. The only goal came 15 minutes from the end with cross from the right, sent over by Leon Smith for Connor Harbridge, to ably meet the ball with his head and find the back of the net.

The Mighty Chertsey Town

We had a couple of late scares, our only ones of the game. One with second half goalkeeper Nick Bennett pulling off a full length save from a shot at distance, and the same player smothering the ball when only he stood between an Ascot forward and a good chance of an equaliser being struck.

Curfews

Chertsey Town Football Club's nickname is The Curfews. Most likely first coined at the club's founding, it is derived from the Curfew bell, one of eight bells that hang in the nearby parish church of St Peter's. The oldest bell, the fifth, was cast in the fourteenth century and comes from the old Abbey of Chertsey, though nowadays a more modern bell, the fourth, from the eighteenth century is used for the Curfew instead. The Curfew has rung out for over 500 years and is still rung today through the autumn and winter on weekday evenings at 8pm, between Michaelmas (29th September) and Lady Day (25th March).

Thursday 26th July – Friendly   Chertsey Town 0 Egham Town 0

Although goalless, this was a very competitive workout with our Isthmian Division One neighbours. The nearest a goal came was when Aaron Smith rounded the Egham Town 'keeper, but his strike lacked velocity and the ball was cleared from the line by a back pedalling defender. Nick Jupp did well for us at the other end by making a couple of significant saves from his custodian position.

Nick Jupp

Chertsey's first choice goalkeeper "had been out of the game for a few years pretty much retired due to a ruptured ACL [anterior cruciate ligament] but I got the call from Dave Anderson to come down and I liked what I saw. I'd played for Dave and with a few of the lads at Harrow which helped. My parents have owned a flooring shop in Chertsey high street for 26 years and so the area is very familiar to me and they were happy that I signed." Nick's Jupp's previous clubs were Shepshed Dynamo, Aldershot Town, Barnet and St Albans City.

His acrobatic, crucial saves throughout the season were a massive contribution to the Club's clean sheet record. In the FA Vase Final programme Kevin Maclaren says Nick's "a player we're fortunate to have here. His shot-stopping ability is unbelievable and his kicking is second to none. He's got a dry sense of humour and makes everyone laugh."

Saturday 28th July – Friendly   Chertsey Town 2 Harrow Borough 2
Visitors Harrow Borough of the Southern League Premier Division may have hit two goals, but they were both fired in from the penalty spot after contentious decisions. Ours were scored in open play with young Craig Ferguson finding the net with a shot across the goal face in the first half, which was then pulled back by the interval, and Leon Smith in the second, which was also neutralised.

Quill Quip

So we are off to another season of moans, but also one of great promise. My philosophy of the club tucking in, as it were, during fallow years so that we can be ready for more abundant times looks like to be bearing fruit. I will be hanging on to my hat this season. I hope more numbers than in the recent past will join me in looking forward to stepping out on the front foot for a change.

Not much has changed at the club, but a lot has changed! That might be a contradiction of terms, but what I mean is that, although a hurricane of modifications has swept through both the material fabric of the ground, and the playing squad with its dressing room force of back up management, the same community philosophy of club life continues.

The Mighty Chertsey Town

> No-one has departed from the committee but in fact it has been enhanced with additional bods. In noting there are now twenty of us, I suspect we have the largest executive, certainly in this league, but even perhaps in the country at our level of football. Let's hope it can be made to work; there certainly is great potential.

Chris Gay, the author of the match reports, Qill Quip and From the Secretary's Quill, is one of the unpaid, unsung heroes of non-league football. He has been supporting Chertsey Town for 60 years. "I got interested in football in my early teens and was persuaded to see Chertsey Town in 1959 by my next door neighbour, and was hooked!" A stint as the Club's Secretary in the 1960s was followed by several years serving football as a referee. In 1974 he hung up his boots and returned to Chertsey Town to offer his secretarial services again. Working in London, raising a family and travelling from his home 12 miles from Chertsey, "We had to move further out as we couldn't find anywhere we could afford in Chertsey", yet finding the time to undertake the onerous paperwork (he also produces the matchday programme), he is a cog typical in all non-league clubs that keeps the wheels of non–league football turning.

Many years ago I met with friends for a picnic at Avebury Standing Stones and, having parked my car in the village's carpark beside a recreation ground, I paused to watch a village football match played out against the backdrop of endless rolling fields and windswept plain and I thought of the time and effort that goes into staging such matches for no remuneration. Replicated throughout the country in scruffy concrete surrounds and green fields alike, without the Chris Gays of this world non-league football simply would not function.

Chris had four goals for the Club at the start of the 2018-2019 season:
- winning a league title
- a Wembley appearance
- having a first round FA Cup away tie against a football league club
- becoming an adequately funded club.

The football season and the first of Dave Rayner and Chris Gay's ambitions for the club started in earnest on Saturday 4th August with a 2-1 away win at Camberley. Jamie Hoppitt of Camberley Town put his side into the lead on 39 minutes. Chertsey replied on 55 minutes through Dale Binns, then Sam Murphy hit the winner on 74 minutes.

The following Tuesday, 7th August, Hanworth Villa were dispatched at home by a solitary Dale Binns goal on 43 minutes.

On Saturday 11th August Chertsey's assault on the third of Dave Rayner and Chris Gay's ambitions began. And ended abruptly.

Saturday 11th August 2018 – FA Cup   Arundel 4 Chertsey Town 1
Chertsey reached the interval one down despite having the lion's share of possession. The one goal deficit turned into two three minutes into the second half but still we kept plugging away. Chances aplenty came and went to pull the game round but we failed to stop effective counter attacks when pressing up field. We fell further behind on 65 minutes but got one back on ninety after Leon Smith latched on to a through ball and fired past the home 'keeper before a further goal was conceded in stoppage time to add to our misery.

Dave Rayner's "low point with Chertsey was Arundel away in the FA Cup. The team had not played together much, with more new players coming in. We had a few more additions to make to strengthen the squad. While it was understandable, it was disappointing to go out so early in the FA Cup as I'd wanted us to get further in that competition. And after that cup defeat we went on to win eight league games in a row!"

The defeat to Arundel for Mark Turner "felt we were a million miles off winning the league. But on the way home I thought it might have done us a favour as there were other cup competitions coming up in addition to the league and had we gone two or three rounds more in the FA Cup it would have put pressure on us later with postponed league matches. Our FA Cup exit turned out to be a blessing in disguise as towards the end of the season league matches postponed to the Vase games were coming at a rate of three a week."

Michael Peacock too rates losing at Arundel the lowest point of the season "with a poor performance, although this may have been a blessing now knowing how the season ended up!"

The defeat to Arundel was a shock result. The equivalent in the 2018-2019 FA Cup would have been if Huddersfield Town had played and knocked out Manchester City in the third round. Arundel were playing in the Southern Combination Premier Division, a parallel league to Chertsey Town's, but the 2018-2019 season proved to be one in Arundel's history books they would rather forget as they ended the season with relegation to Step 6 of non-league football, to the Southern Combination Division 1.

The football league structure is an uneven pyramid shape set out in a number of steps. The Premiership is Step 1 of the Football League, the Championship is Step 2, the English Football League One is Step 3 and the English Football

League Two is Step 4. Below that lies the National League (formerly known as the Conference) which is both Step 5 of the Football League and Step 1 of non-league football. Down to this point the top five divisions form a tower rather than a pyramid as there is only a single division at each level.

The shape then starts to pan out into a pyramid proper with Step 6 of the Football League/Step 2 of non-league football consisting of two divisions, National League North and National League South. Below this at Step 7 (Football League)/Step 3 (non-league) lie four leagues alongside each other: the Isthmian League, the Norther Premier League, the Southern League Central and the Southern League South.

Below that the pyramid becomes a little uneven. While you might expect eight leagues in Step 8 (Football League)/Step 4 (non-league), in the 2019-2020 season there are still only seven: Isthmian League South Central, Isthmian League North, Isthmian League South East, Northern Premier League South East, Northern Premier League North West, Southern League Central and Southern League South. The Football Association is working towards the introduction of an eighth league at this level from the 2020-2021 season onwards to encompass clubs from the north-east of England.

Fourteen leagues lie at Step 9 (Football League)/Step 5 (non-league) including the Combined Counties Premier and the Southern Combination Premier. Beyond this are further steps with ever increasing numbers of leagues at each step and ultimately leagues comprising clubs like the humble village team I saw at Avebury all those years ago.

With the FA Cup defeat it was back to that old football cliché, "We're concentrating on the league," which Chertsey Town proceeded to do in style.

The Mighty Chertsey Town

Saturday 18th August – CC League Chertsey Town 4
Raynes Park Vale 1

It took less than a minute to shrug off the disappointment of the previous week's FA Cup demise. Defender Lewis Jackson fired us into the lead in our first Saturday home match of the season, a Combined Counties League encounter with newly promoted Raynes Park Vale. The visitors put up a spirited performance but were always chasing the game from that initial moment.

We demonstrated class at times but showed that there was still more in the tank to come. Even so, we recorded the biggest win of the day in the competition to remain one of three sides with one hundred per cent records. The final score line might have been even more emphatic had a penalty kick, awarded late in the game for a raised hand, been put away by John Pomroy, but his strike was comfortably saved, to become only a footnote to a contest already decided.

It was the conceding of free kicks that was Vale's initial undoing. The first goal was converted by Jackson off a free kick, but the middle man was cut out when Andy Crossley, with our second, directly found the top corner of the Raynes Park Vale net from 20 yards after Pomroy was upended at the edge of the box. Goalkeeper Reece Turner stood no chance.

It might have seemed that the result now would be a foregone conclusion but the visitors struck back seven minutes later. It was a dreadful goal to concede as far as we were concerned. The defence was all at sea; more like an ocean. It allowed our visitors to sail in with a couple of ten yard passes that ended with the unattended Jack Williamson turning the ball in giving Nick Jupp no means to retrieve the situation.

The goal gave heart and Vale gave as good as they got but with no obvious chances being created at either end by the time the interval arrived. Seven players, of the eleven that kicked off for us, were new to the club this season so it is only natural that the synchromesh between the gears have not yet fully bedded in but confidence was in the Alwyns Lane air at the break.

That confidence was justified after half time. Pomroy might have increased the lead but his header went wide off supply from Dave Taylor, collected from a raking midfield pass. Leon Smith then came on for Lewis Driver. Very soon after the switch, on 66 minutes, we stretched the lead to two goals. From another dead ball scene, this time a corner kick on the right, Michael Peacock volleyed the ball home from ten yards.

It took another six minutes before another strike made its mark. The simplicity of the lead up is an exciting prospect for supporters if this sort of football can be achieved on a regular basis as sweeping passes just shredded the Vale defence. It was finished off with a Crossley cross and a no nonsense Smith header into the net.

It was not to be Pomroy's day for another chance went a begging, along with the penalty miss but he is at last getting support once more so future goals look like to flow once more. Meanwhile, the defence was well organised, but for the one first half lapse, but a further goal might have been conceded late on with James Curran for the visitors looked dangerous when meeting the ball on the far post but each time was thwarted. Michael Kinsella, off the bench, might have also entered the score sheet with a powerful header that Curran parried.

Lewis Jackson

The scorer of Chertsey's first goal against Raynes Park Vale, Lewis Jackson was a close season signing from Cobham. Playing central midfield in the friendlies he moved to right back for the season proper. Roommate of the long distance away trips later in the season, Michael Kinsella calls him "An all-round top bloke and a very good player. Underrated in my opinion." Lewis, Kevin Maclaren comments in the FA Vase Final programme, "Gives the team a boost when he's on the pitch."

The Mighty Chertsey Town

Saturday 25th August – CC League   Southall 0 Chertsey Town 1

The side maintained its one hundred percent league record to go second in the table in our Combined Counties League fixture at Ashford Town's ground, the new home for Southall, but it was a close run thing. It was not so much a danger of us losing the game for goalkeeper Lewis Gallifent was not required to make one significant save. It was the clock that became the real enemy, but was overcome three minutes into stoppage time when the only goal, and winner, was secured.

The Bank Holiday weekend put paid to key elements of our front rank squad. 'Keeper Nick Jupp and striker Dale Binns were both unavailable. The gap allowed last term's Under 18 side prospect Connor Harbridge a chance to show his wares but unfortunately for him, he tweaked a groin strain and was replaced at half time by Leon Smith.

The match itself was no classic. Flowing football was not the order of the day with the condition of the playing surface making its contribution. We were put under pressure in the opening minutes, but tight defending denied Southall any openings. In fact the home side struggled to conjure any meaningful shots on goal. Strikes were either blocked by the outfield, fired straight at Gallifent or, more frequently, blasted high and wide from distance.

On the other hand, our far fewer direct attempts at goal had more potency, commencing with a 25-yard free kick in the 14th minute, delivered by Andy Crossley who had been brought down. The delivery stretched goalkeeper Rory Mullane into a full length save that generated a trio of corner kicks. Play was somewhat disjointed, not helped by too many petty fouls, mainly in the midfield, mainly with us being the culprits, but without being sinister or malice. It did though draw two persistent misconduct yellow cards from the referee.

The second half held better fare as far as attractive football was

Alice Graysharp with Chris Gay

concerned, but only by a whisker. Southall became even less of a threat from then on. We increased opportunities to engineer an advantage but could not make a series of half chances count. Just a few minutes after the turnaround saw a weak off-balance stab at goal from Smith. Lewis Driver fired over from a good position after being put in by Sam Murphy. Driver then headed a yard wide off a right wing cross as the pace of our game increased.

John Pomroy came on late for Driver to try a different angle against a well regimented Southall defence and it was a knocked down off his chest after a Kevin Maclaren pass in the middle that saw the ball reach Smith. He was somewhat crowded out in the middle of the penalty area but made enough of a nuisance of himself for the ball to find Dave Taylor who calmly 'passed' the ball into the net with just one full back in the goalmouth to stop its flight and Mullane stuck in no man's land.

The winner came well into stoppage time but there was still plenty of the game left to create nervousness, not from the players who saw out the remaining five minutes without any major scares, but from the travelling crowd who appreciated the three point afternoon's entertainment, even if the quality had not quite yet made the grade.

Tuesday 28th August – CC League   Knaphill 0 Chertsey Town 4

A successive clean sheet performance against the previously 'bogie' hosts of Knaphill hoisted us further up the table in what was initially a feisty encounter but in the end had more the air of a meaningless friendly match. The change in atmosphere came in stages, marked by the goals as well as two red card dismissals that left the Woking based side with nine players on the park at the 90-minute mark.

Both sides displayed uncompromising steel in the first half with tackles that would have had TV's Minder Terry McCann's

The Mighty Chertsey Town

'tasty' epithet well deserved. It was a case of establishing a hierarchy, one that went the way of us visitors. One Town yellow was conceded as was one Knappers' yellow and one red in the first half with referee Scott Crowhurst managing to eventually calm the situation.

There was football in between; plenty of it, but not so much in front of goal initially. We bagged all of what was on offer with the first coming on 14 minutes in bizarre fashion. Michael Kinsella released the ball from a deep position, high over all outfield players. It looked like possession would pass to Knaphill but goalkeeper Luke Skinner misjudged the bounce as he advanced to the edge of his area and over his head it went. Leon Smith took the laurels in a race to get to the wayward ball and tickled it into the net. Kinsella's assist will be remembered for quite some time.

Knaphill looked as if they were about to reply but Nick Jupp saved with his outstretched legs as Felix Ahorlu sent him the wrong way after bearing down from the right. Smith had another chance to score but this time Skinner did his job to block. Soon after, George Rowley received his marching orders for a flying two footed effort.

The second half concentrated football minds more than the distractions that marred the first, and it was us that got in first. It was seven minutes after the break from where Andy Crossley, on the left, arched the ball into high orbit to the far post. Sam Murphy was on station and celebrated his industrious performance with a half volley strike that Skinner was not able to grab cleanly as the missile found its target for a two-goal lead.

We were well in the ascendancy during most of the second period. Smith broke through, but, Skinner had the upper hand this time in the one to one contest. Murphy assumed good wide positions to cut the ball back to in rushing prospective strikers with Kevin Maclaren narrowly firing the missile over and full back Lewis Jackson shooting wide as the most memorable efforts.

Craig Ferguson came on for Crossley for a like for like exchange. The home side still had ambitions of turning the game round when Jupp was called upon to block off Aserick Samuels who found a good position from a low left-wing cross. However, we were the side to strike next. Soon after, on 65 minutes in fact, a surging run by Lewis Driver set up a penalty kick after Skinner mistimed an attempt at snatching at the ball.

The spot kick was leathered away by Murphy. It was just as well he put power into the shot as the goalkeeper got a touch. With three goals the difference and 25 minutes remaining, the fire went out of Knaphill's challenge, but with one exemption when Jupp executed an acrobatic defence against a fiercely driven strike at close range. But it was at the other end that further pain was inflicted.

The fourth came after Connor Maclaren came on to mark his Chertsey Town debut, and mark it he did with a stunning goal. A throw found its way to him just outside of the box. From there, he released an out swinging shot that found the top corner of the net. The situation seemed to rile Knaphill's Timmy Taylor who remonstrated to the referee in a sustained manner and so was eventually sent to the stands.

We had plenty of space to knock the ball about with almost too deliberate ease. A powerful strike by Ferguson was tipped over and one from Murphy was saved as we completed the job to climb to the top of the table; a feat that has not been done for many a year.

Michael Kinsella

The provider of the spectacular assist for Chertsey's first goal against Knaphill, Michael joined Chertsey Town from Bedfont Sports in March 2018 "due to Dave Anderson taking over." Instrumental in Chertsey's rise to the top of the league, he was dealt a rotten hand in March 2019 with a leg fracture that took him out of the final run in. A vastly experienced central defender, having also played for CB Hounslow, Harrow Borough and as team captain at North Greenford United, it is to his credit that once he was up and hobbling he was to be seen at matches urging the team on and showing a positive spirit to the supporters. Ruled out of the Vase semi-final, Michael was asked "if I wanted to commentate for Live Sports FM and I did. Really enjoyed it." Kevin Maclaren's view in the FA Vase Final programme of Michael's attitude is, "Outstanding. Always gives you 100 per cent and is a player you want with you in the trenches."

August Quill Quip

This season is building up to be more inspirational than most. No doubt we will have some lows along with the highs and it will be interesting to see how much 'luck' we can generate, especially with refereeing decisions which, as we all know, can often be contentious, be it because an 'incident' is misread by those on the park, or us experts viewing from the spectator barrier.

I veer towards that thought after our week upon week [World Cup] experiences in Russia this summer past when the Video Assistant Referee (VAR) system produced as much controversy as it was supposed to avoid. We will not have the luxury of instantly reviewing key moments at our level of football but I doubt if we will feel deprived as plenty of 'live' opinion dominates our game.

The distance between top flight football and that at our level seems to becoming ever wider. The notion to operate football as one, from the park to national stadiums, and at all levels has become nigh on impossible.

Innovation can come from non-league football. I can write of two in my time that emanated from within Isthmian circles.

> The idea to give the option of an indirect free kick when the ball went out of play (to potentially save time, but had the opposite effect) failed, but three points, instead of two, for a win (to encourage attacking play) was a spectacular success.
>
> VAR has, for me, confirmed the notion that, whatever aids are introduced to make decisions 'right,' it will never eliminate opinion and interpretation. Long may that notion reign as we continue here at Alwyns Lane with SAR; the 'Supporter Assisting Referee,' system!

The approach of the autumn equinox was dominated by cup games – two rounds of the FA Vase and one of the League Cup.

Chertsey Town's foray into the FA Vase began on 1st September at home to Woodley United of the Hellenic Football League's Division One East. The match on paper should have been an easy win, a Step 6 club away to a team mostly comprised of higher league-experienced players. However, the Berkshire club gave Chertsey something of a run for their money, netting two goals but were ultimately not a match for Chertsey's four goals divided between Pomroy (2), Smith and Guentchev.

Sandwiched between cup games was the meat of the league campaign.

Saturday 8th September – CC League Chertsey Town 3 Horley Town 1

We confirmed our top spot with a comfortable victory over visitors Horley Town. The win stretched the 100% record to six games. The main downer of the afternoon though was the fracture sustained by Horley's Andy Hall who left the ground in the back of an ambulance after emerging from an uncontentious clash.

The travellers did not have a great afternoon in other directions either. Striker Karl Parker received two yellow cards, the

The Mighty Chertsey Town

second on 66 minutes, which reduced his side to ten men, but the damage had already been done by then. There looked very little chance of a comeback despite scoring a goal and showing up well in the second period. Even so, the one man deficit did not seem to make much difference.

Goalkeeper Nick Jupp was unavailable so 18-year-old Lewis Gallifent stepped up for the second time this season. He was protected well, but with one fatal exception. Lewis Driver returned after illness but Danny Bennell was unavailable. Mason Welch-Turner began his three match ban after the red of the previous week. Scott Cousins was drafted in at left back to replace Leon Smith, and John Pomroy dropped to the bench.

Horley Town began with confidence and might well have taken an early lead when the ball flashed across our crowded goalmouth, but no-one got a touch. Any sort of contact from any player would surely have seen the ball crash into the net. The let off was all we needed as we began to assert ourselves. The result put us a goal to the good. It came on 12 minutes when the ball bounced up nicely for Andy Crossley who, from 20 yards, unleashed a half volley strike that gave George Hyde in goal no chance. In reply six minutes later, Horley's Ben King fired the ball from distance but it went straight at Gallifent who gathered comfortably.

Shots directed at goal from well outside the respective penalty areas by both sides was a feature of the first half but only one was effective. We found the net twice more before the break, one from inside and another, outside the box. But before those successes, Crossley might have increased our lead when a Dave Taylor cross bounced awkwardly in front of Crossley so that he could only hook the ball over despite being inside the six yard area.

That miss was soon forgotten when, in the 23rd minute, an express train run by Crossley was halted just inside the box resulting in a penalty kick. Dale Binns stepped up and sent the 'keeper the wrong way. It was looking now all too easy as number three was secured just ten minutes later. Lubo Guentchev snatched his second goal in two outings. It came from a weak headed clearance attempt. He collected the ball 25 yards out and fired the well aimed strike ball home low and hard past Hyde who tried his best at full length.

Horley Town were being steam rollered at this point but despite our dominance no more goals came. The three decisive strikes thus came in the first half hour.

Horley Town will most likely believe they had the edge after the break but we played well within ourselves, particularly in defence which performed as one unit despite having a debutante in Cousins on station. One lapse did occur however. It arrived on the hour, too late to make a real impact, but at least gave the visitors some heart for when the two sides meet again, ten days hence. A gaping hole appeared centrally just inside the Curfew box. King exploited the opening when receiving the ball from his left to fire a powerful strike from 12 yards that Gallifent got a touch to but not enough to prevent hearing the net bulge behind him.

What with the unfortunate injury, the Parker dismissal and Chertsey in a comfortable position, the game rather lost its way. Binns tried, after making good progress, a cheeky lob that Hyde just managed to tip over together with a late shot across the bows from the same player. This was balanced at the other end with a volley, close in by Jack Poplett, that was skied.

Effectively, the game was done and dusted in the first third. It always provides extra excitement when the main action happens in the latter stages of any exchange. It does not always happen but the end result, for us on this occasion, must be seen as just as satisfying.

Andy Crossley

The scorer of the first goal against Horley Town, Andy Crossley is a veteran of non-league football at only 25. His early years were nurtured at Farncombe Youth Football Club near Godalming. Joining Chertsey Town at 16, he says he's "loved the club ever since." Initially playing for the Under 18s, he made his first team debut in August 2010 as a 17-year-old.

Andy subsequently played for Farnborough, Egham Town and Godalming Town, returning to Chertsey Town in November 2014. A spell followed at Westfield, then he signed for Chertsey a third time in the summer of 2018. He just can't keep away and has made over 250 appearances for Chertsey Town. In the FA Vase Final programme Kevin Maclaren views Andy as "one of our more underrated players. Andy quietly goes about his business but consistently pops up with assists and goals. He's deadly from set pieces. A very likeable lad."

Next up was the second fixture of the FA Vase competition.

**Saturday 15th September – FA Vase 1st Qualifying   Tadley Calleva 0
                                                     Chertsey Town 1**

Grind, grind, and more grind. That is what it took to take this FA Vase tie at third placed Wessex League side Tadley Calleva at their rural ground a few miles north of Basingstoke. The win not only avenged the defeat suffered by this same side three years previous, but also recorded our second Vase win for the season, a feat that has not occurred for nine long years.

Although departing from the setting with a victory under our belt, we will play better than was seen in this game and lose. The dry scratchy playing surface played a part in restricting the game to just the one goal, but in fairness, the other factor was the opposition who made a real contest of the tie and were devastated to have conceded in stoppage time.

Alice Graysharp with Chris Gay

They were not that devastated at the time for, despite us scoring so late in the game, our guests came within a whisper, or should it have been a good shout, of scoring an equaliser. It took a flying one handed save from Nick Jupp to deny a close range effort from a Tadley attacker.

Both sides had periods of ascendancy; it could hardly be called dominance. The home side were effective in breaking out from the midfield with long straiking passes, often sent to the right flank to their number nine, Cameron George to sprint after and collect. Although he had a couple of nibbles, he was bottled up in the main by the shadowing Michael Kinsella.

Our way was to construct more networked passes, but space was frequently found on the left for Dale Binns to exploit. His distribution, however, was not on the button this day and fewer chances than his usual were set up. He was not the only one though to misplace passes. This led to few goal openings at either end. The first half saw Calleva perhaps enjoying more half chances than ourselves, but we had the best opportunities.

Both of these fell to Lubo Guentchev. The first, on ten minutes, saw him a toe away from beating Sean O'Brien, but the goalkeeper, at the second juggled attempt won the contest. The next came just before the break after Andy Crossley collected from Binns and centred, but Guentchev, centrally placed 15 yards out and O'Brien off beam, fired straight at a lone goal line defender.

If the first half could be said to be equally balanced, the second went narrowly in our favour, but still without enough penetration to make a real difference, and it was the home side that could have slid into the lead. The action came eleven minutes after the turnaround when a long range header from Paul Coventry might have crept in. It did not, in the same way a low curling Guentchev effort failed in rounding the far post.

The Mighty Chertsey Town

Both sides looked able to spring the trap despite less than clear cut chances being created. We had a better grip but the home side was well organised and ready to pose danger. The ominous spectre of extra time though was rising in line with nerves on the touch line. One slip in these latter stages would spell doom; and so it happened!

A free kick for a push was award to us, some 30 yards out. A sneaky quick one was taken by Leon Smith, on for the replaced John Pomroy. It was collected by Guentchev who cut across to Tadley penalty area to give himself room. This achieved, the attacker wiped away thoughts of first half misses by sweeping the ball past O'Brien, three minutes into stoppage time.

The home side threw everything into the remaining three minutes and almost pulled off a thundering equaliser inside the crowded penalty area, but the Jupp left hand and leap saved the day to put halt the Hampshire side in its tracks. The save ensured we entered the hat for the impending first round draw and the home side could resume their prime quest for league points.

John Waghorne, Chertsey's Under 18s manager, picks out the FA Vase away game at Tadley Calleva as his match of the season because it was such a crucial match for the first team. "Their pitch was poor due to the lack of water and was breaking up on the wings and they were a decent side, we scored late on when extra time was looming and only a fingertip save in the dying seconds by Nick Jupp prevented extra time."

Next up was Chertsey's first fixture in the League Cup, a midweek match away to Horley Town on 18th September. Chertsey came out 1-0 winners courtesy of John Pomroy.

John Pomroy
The scorer of the only goal against Horley Town, John Pomroy is no stranger to goalscoring for Chertsey Town. He joined Chertsey Town in 2000 from Fulham (with whom he was an apprentice and whose scores he looks out for) and then Aldershot, "to play regular first team football." He has also played for Walton & Hersham, Lewes, Bognor Regis Town and Egham Town during his football career. Returning to Chertsey Town for his fourth spell in 2011, he has made over 650 appearances for Chertsey Town and has scored 347 goals. The supporters have their own song for him, "John Pomroy is a legend…"

For his team captain Kevin Maclaren, John Pomroy deserves a special mention. "What's impressed me most about him is his attitude and the way he's been with new players coming into his club. There hasn't been one ounce of resentment for not playing as many games as he would like. He's been supportive, encouraging and always acted in the best interests of the team."

Overnight trips' roommate Andy Crossley confirms John Pomroy's selfless attitude. "Like the fans sing, he truly is a legend. He has been fantastic this season at bringing the squad together and still scoring big goals. Pommers is a top guy and a brilliant footballer. Pommers' character was summed up for me when he told me the day before the Vase Final at Wembley that if he could guarantee we win and he didn't play one minute he would take it straight away… That says all you need to know about him."

In the FA Vase Final programme Kevin Maclaren sums up. "John is a true club legend. He's a lovely bloke."

SUMMER 2018

Director of Football 2018-2019 Dave Rayner

Manager 2018-2019 Dave Anderson

The Mighty Chertsey Town

Club Secretary Chris Gay (on right, with Philip Hammond former MP for Runnymede and Weybridge)

Club Official Photographer Andy Pearson

Alice Graysharp with Chris Gay

Mason Welch-Turner (left) and Commercial Manager 2018-2019 Mark Turner

(L to R) Match Secretary Sue Powers, Lubomir Guentchev, Club Secretary Chris Gay (partially obscured), Club Chairman 2018-2019 Steve Powers and Mason Welch-Turner

The Mighty Chertsey Town

Dale Binns (in yellow)

Goalkeeper Nick Jupp in action

Lewis Jackson

Michael Kinsella

Andy Crossley

John Pomroy (far right) scoring one of
his 347 goals, against Southall

The John Pomroy banner

AUTUMN 2018

Saturday 22nd September – CC League   Chertsey Town 2 Cobham 1

As wide apart as the Combined Counties League standings between the two sides were on paper, there often looked little to choose between the teams for substantial chunks of the game. But there was a difference, and it pulled us through to collect the full points once more.

On this showing, newly promoted Cobham will not be languishing in the nether regions of the table for long. Their tough programme of games up to that point are to give way to easier opposition so that this narrow Chertsey win, will in time, be put into better perspective.

One, among many striking features of this season, is the settled look to the team, especially in defence. Apart from the number three shirt, the others, up to seven, is almost a given. There is a bit of movement in the forward line but overall, it can confidently be said that we have a settled side.

It has been a feature of our games that periods of unspectacular football, be it nonetheless solid, give a balanced look to contests, but then the side turns it on for a while, gets the required goal, or goals, then subsides into its former state.

Something akin to that scenario occurred in this game. Cobham had a very lively start and could have created an upset in only the second minute with a half chance, but one that was spurned by Chris Davis.

We also had an early opportunity to impose on the game. Dale Binns forged through on the right, to win a corner kick, from which Michael Peacock's header although looking convincing enough, nonetheless, shot wide. The move was initiated by Sam Murphy who possibly had his most influential game in our colours to date.

Cobham's bright beginnings saw fruit on seven minutes. Gary Abisogun did very well to keep possession in our crowded penalty area. He eventually let go with a shot and got lucky, perhaps as a reward for his persistence. His comfortable looking goal effort clipped a back heel en route, diverting the ball to just inside the post.

Another penetrating Binns run set up the equaliser. It came in the 21st minute with Lubo Guentchev striking the ball first time with the outside of his foot giving Lee Norman in goal no chance.

Mo Diakite, for the visitors, generated a comfortable save from Nick Jupp in goal almost on the hour and something similar was set up by the same player late in the game. These were the only two moments that looked remotely like an upset would happen.

By then, we had taken the lead with Murphy capping his contribution with a goal on 58 minutes to effectively put the game to bed at that point. The defence was too wily to allow lightning to strike twice in the exchange. Cobham continued to give a spirited response but the feeling that we were not going to let slip our place at the top of the league table was borne out, come the 90 minutes.

Lubomir Guentchev

The scorer of Chertsey's first goal against Cobham, Lubo is a Bulgarian born striker who is now mainly based in England. He has played for Yantra Polski Trambesh in Bulgaria's top flight and was an Under 23 international. He has also played in Germany and, in England, for Hendon and Lowestoft Town. Kevin Maclaren played with him at Hendon. In the FA Vase Final programme Kevin Maclaren notes that "Dad Boncho played at the 1994 World Cup." Of Lubo, Maclaren reveals, "We call him 'the Rolls Royce'."

Alice Graysharp with Chris Gay

**Saturday 29th September – CC League   Sutton Common Rovers 1
Chertsey Town 1**

We dropped our first league points of the season with a result that could have gone either way but might also have followed the familiar pattern of us hitting a stoppage time winner. Had the late flurry that set up a close range shot at Rovers' goalkeeper been sent to his side and not directly at him, a more productive end would have ensued. As it was, all our main rivals fell by the wayside so that the position in the table was, ironically, even more secure after of the day's programme of matches.

Three players were taken out of the equation by representing England in Portugal in a six a side tournament. This prompted the return of defender Mason Welch-Turner after suspension, the midfield inclusion of Connor Maclaren for his first league start of the season, and the debut of prolific striker Jake Baxter, newly signed from Hartley Wintney. It could hardly be said that these players were there to fill the gaps, but more that the squad has quality in depth.

The game, played in bright, warm sunshine on Sutton United's artificial surface, might have suited both sides for differing reasons. The host team will have been more used to the pace of the ball but much of our game currently relies on close order ball skills. The result was that neither side could have been said to richly deserve all three points. They both had their moments, but mainly in the midfield; there was very little to separate the sides.

We showed more menace in the first half, especially in the early stages. It took a good quarter of an hour before Rovers mounted any real attack, and that ended with a comfortable Nick Jupp save off a 25-yard free kick. Although we had the initiative, the home defence held firm, a constant pattern at both ends throughout the exchange. But a breakthrough was achieved; it came in the 34th minute after a period of Chertsey pressure.

The Mighty Chertsey Town

Dale Binns was posing his usual problems for the opposition wide on his right. He made progress, crossed the ball for Baxter. A moment of ball protection and adjustment deep in the Sutton penalty area then saw him set up Andy Crossley who calmly slotted the ball home from some ten yards. Four minutes later, with us enjoying our best moments, Binns came closest to forcing a second with a 25-yard shot that skimmed the top of the net as top spin took a grip, but not strongly enough.

A double half time substitution by the home side and a more attacking formation loosened the Rovers leash and the marginal honours claimed by us in the first half were snatched by the home side. It took just five minutes of this new offence for the equaliser to be registered. A classic deep left-wing delivery from Jordan Gallagher found the head of former Curfews' favourite Phil Page who found the golden touch, and the back of our net.

The goal gave way to additional Sutton confidence, but as in the first half at the other end, no telling opportunities could be forged out from strong defending. It was not all one way though as Welch-Turner forced a full length save from Ollie Ellaway in goal after the ball had been robbed from tangled full back's feet. Jupp then had to block a Sutton Common goal attempt on 79 minutes.

But we became the strongest in the latter stages with Baxter showing what a good catch he will prove to be, with plenty of promise from his late efforts. He clipped the ball over at an angle off a corner, then two minutes later, tried to curl another in off a deep cross. This was followed by another attempt with a glancing header that, in truth was never going to strike home, but still showed promise.

Such was our confidence at this point that even full back Lewis Jackson joined in with the attack and it was his strike, admittedly in a tight situation, that was too accurate and found the body of Ellaway instead of the intention to bypass a despairing outstretched arm. The two points dropped will only have disappointed the statisticians, wanting to see how many straight wins we could produce. But it has to be said that the draw was a satisfying result that still kept us clear on the top rung of the ladder.

Connor Maclaren

Connor Maclaren, enjoying his full debut for Chertsey against Sutton Common Rovers, signed for Chertsey in 2018 after a year out of football. He was connected as a youth with Chelsea and Millwall and then had spells at Cobham, Banstead Athletic and Epsom & Ewell. His older brother Kevin Maclaren describes him in the FA Vase Final programme as having "put in some very good performances" in a couple of rounds in the Vase. Connor's season was later marred by illness. "He's also," reveals big brother, "the singer of the group!"

September Quill Quip

Once upon a time there was a great fairy tale scribe called Hans Christian Andersen. The renowned author penned many tales, mostly dark and with morals attached, despite children being the primary targets. One of these stories, The Ugly Duckling, occurred to me last week when thinking about this past summer at Alwyns Lane. The story of a tatty and disregarded youngster being transformed when no-one was around, into a beautiful adolescent is well known. I almost wrote the word 'graceful' when trying to weld together that story and what has happened recently, but it takes that word just a bit too far!

Well, we all know what is said about a swan. It may look as if it is effortlessly gliding about a placid stretch of water, but in fact its webbed feet are going ten to the dozen as it battles against

The Mighty Chertsey Town

the unnoticed current beneath the surface. You could say that something like that is happening at Chertsey Town.

Dave Rayner has put great resources into returning the ground back to its former self (and beyond), but in doing that, it still requires almost daily attention to keep on top. The simple task of sweeping up and then emptying the bins does not happen by itself. Paid contractors do not do the task for us. There is a task list of 34 basic items that need to be tamed by committee members on a weekly basis. Those committee members are, as at almost all clubs, simple volunteers. Some, like myself, are more dippy than others and jobs not done, or done incorrectly, impact on others.

With poetic spelling licence, we also have our own Anderson on board, working on the reality of attaining the goals for not only our Director of Football (DR) but of us all. Let's do our best to assist him as he takes the lead by turning our drama into a fairy tale of its own by getting us some long cherished silverware back to Alwyns Lane.

Combined Counties League Premier Division
Top 4 – end of September

	P	W	D	L	F	A	Gd	Pts
Chertsey Town	8	7	1	0	18	5	_13_	22
Banstead Athletic	11	4	7	0	16	9	_7_	19
Redhill	9	5	1	3	21	15	_6_	16
Abbey Rangers	8	5	1	2	15	11	_4_	16

Saturday 6th October – CC League **Chertsey Town 3**
Colliers Wood United 0

Our reign at the top of the league table continued after demolishing visitors Colliers Wood United whilst being drenched by severely leaking skies. The win came out of as a controlled performance as could be expected at such a level of competition and was probably our most polished showing of the season. The under pinning of the win could be said to have come from the back line which stayed disciplined throughout the game.

It often felt there was an extra man in defence, such was the effectiveness of cover that was supplied for the rest of the side. It was not just Messrs. Jackson, Bennell, Kinsella and Welch-Turner that were doing their job. This cohesiveness gave licence for the midfield to project probing balls forward so that United were constantly under threat. The visitors gave a good account of themselves but were afforded little opportunity to take anything away with them from soggy Alwyns Lane.

Two key moments, just either side of the interval, confirmed where the points were going. On 44 minutes, United's Ben Anderson, through his speed being the main thorn in our side, burst through but his competent strike was stopped at full length by Nick Jupp. Two minutes after the break, Andy Crossley increased an already established lead, to make the remainder of the game pretty well a foregone conclusion.

An almost full complement was on offer for selection to Dave Anderson at the start of the afternoon. The result was a powerful line up that, for the first time at home, featured recently signed striker Jake Baxter. His inclusion was instantly felt by scoring two of our three goals and setting up the third. Additionally, he linked well, especially with Crossley and a very mobile Lubo Guentchev as the main striking force. It bodes well for the side's future ambitions.

Both of the latter had early strikes but then the defence, for two or three minutes around the quarter of an hour mark, seemed to lose concentration and might have paid the price in a torrid period. Although no outright chances were allowed in consequence, the moment was a wakeup call which was heeded.

The Mighty Chertsey Town

Baxter had a goal effort blocked after more good linkage work with Guentchev, and both Crossley and Michael Kinsella had goes at goal, but the breakthrough came on 34 minutes when a foraging run by Crossley on the left was halted after Owen Davies stuck out a hand to stop the ball going past. The penalty area was the location so, from the spot, Baxter confidently blasted the ball home to give what was to become a slender half time advantage.

Two minutes into the second half saw left wing movement by Baxter. He knocked the ball inside, to be collected by Crossley who tucked it away from eight yards for goal number two. The number was up now for Colliers Wood United but they kept hope alive by showing a competitive edge, but without reward. The mid period substitution of Crossley might have raised a faint hope with straws being grasped, but when it is Dale Binns coming on, a whiff of realism was soon forged.

A period of United frustration earned them two yellow dissent cards. Anderson's speed again got him into a good position but he put his shot wide. The stuffing was finally knocked out of Wood's challenge with our third goal midway through the half. Guentchev, by using speed as he cut in from the right, made the goal by getting past goalkeeper Sean Fallon. The ball might, or might not have crossed the line as defenders honed in, but Baxter made sure with a touch over, almost from within the net.

We always looked good for another netting but it never came. Binns came the closest with a 30-yard strike that had Fallon working at full stretch. Dave Taylor came off the bench for Baxter but only lasted a few minutes before badly twisting an ankle, giving John Pomroy fifteen minutes of fun, now that pressure had eased. The likelihood of a late Colliers Wood revival was scant in the extreme as the defence continued doing its job with established efficiency to maintain the eleven-match unbeaten run and a pliable springboard for the following week's crucial FA Vase tie.

Alice Graysharp with Chris Gay

Quill Quip

This Flackwell Heath FA Vase tie today marks one of the more salient moments of each season at Alwyns Lane when we host an FA Vase tie (hopefully not the last). The competition, for clubs at our level, creates a special atmosphere, especially when reaching, say, the fourth round, the last 32. We still have quite a few hurdles to jump before being able to speculate who we might meet in the last sixteen, but anticipation is already vibrating. One of us two sides today though, is soon to be ejected.

At least it will be the result gained on the field of play that will sort out who will be in the hat for Monday's draw. I nearly wrote that the football will be arbiter of victory, but that is not always the case because the dreaded ineligible player charge looms ever larger over us these days; or should I say, looms over me as club secretary, but I am not alone, although I have fallen foul of this situation in the past.

So I will be keeping my fingers crossed over the next few days, commencing at 3.00pm. I am not only hoping for a win on the park, but also to be able to retain any victory gained, within the machinations of our Byzantine competition rules.

Saturday 13th October – FA Vase 1st Round   Chertsey Town 6
Flackwell Heath 1

It is often a classic scenario when the team that scores first with a really early one, then goes on to be heavily defeated. This phenomenon occurred in this FA Vase tie involving mid table Hellenic League opposition. Flackwell Heath went one up in only two minutes, but ended up five goals adrift from our rampant repost. The initial sting was drawn eight minutes after Flackwell's waspish start and from then on the steam roller just rolled on.

The tie turned into a celebration of our grubby recent past transforming itself into a colourful butterfly of the present, and

The Mighty Chertsey Town

potentially the foreseeable future. The football played set up six spectacular goals and a real team spirit with plenty of understanding and confidence to entertain the best home crowd seen for over two seasons. Even neutral spectators would have the extra treat of Flackwell's goal being pretty special too.

Goalkeeper Nick Jupp was on best man duties so Lewis Gallifent was again drafted in. Apart from a slight wobble at the start, he made an assured contribution. It was not any error of his though that the first goal was conceded. Flackwell started like a train and hemmed us into our last third of the park. The overwhelming effect produced a fierce shot that scraped along the cross bar, then the goal from a half clearance by full back Cameron Gray who powered the ball into the top corner.

The remaining line up had a very familiar look with one notable exception that was a highlight of the end game when Dalson Ernesto, from last term's Under 18s side, imprinted his debut with a spot kick goal, justly awarded for his foray that drew a foul. He was told to finish the job by a delighted Dave Anderson, and comfortably did so. Admittedly, Ernesto was given more space that might normally be the case as Flackwell pushed up to try and create the most unlikely reversal of the year, but he exploited the licence to the full.

The introduction of Jake Baxter to the club, two games previous to this exchange, has topped the team's solid, but often unrewarded, efforts. The hattrick he secured was almost half expected; he did not disappoint! The bonus was in the manner of his successes. The first of the trio was forced on ten minutes. A long Gallifent clearance found a right sided Sam Murphy who knocked an early cross into the opposition penalty area. There, Baxter swung at the ball that was slightly behind him. His acrobatic action saw the ball hooked past Hendy Craven in goal.

A Baxter flick soon after led to an Andy Crossley strike that hit the post and off for a goal kick. The respite for the Heathens did not last long. The next back flick goal came from Lubo Guentchev. It was set on 23 minutes when a long throw from Lewis Jackson took one bounce before the booted connection from a dozen yards again defeated Craven.

Our tally increased to three within a few moments of the restart. A ball pumped through the middle was meat and drink to Baxter and he put the ball away from 15 yards. This put one foot through the door to the next round with only 24 minutes gone. Quickfire passing almost set up Connor Maclaren but his feet were not set quite right as he fired at goal but it was another sign that a Chertsey attack might come from any quarter.

It took eleven minutes of the second half to properly confirm that we were to head for Round Two. Kevin Maclaren released a powerful shot at distance. The ball was blocked but brother Connor took up the cudgel, but his shot was this time spilled by Craven. This set up Baxter to clear up. Confidence was further boosted with the three-goal gap as we basically ran Flackwell ragged, not that the visitors were incompetent or unwilling but, on this occasion, just could not keep up.

Crowned by his 81st minute goal, Ernesto's introduction was a revelation as we continued to dominate. The final flurry of defence splitting passes emanating on the left wing was directed inside where Guentchev finished off in style for goal number six with five minutes of play remaining.

Lewis Gallifent

Lewis joined Chertsey Town in March 2018, "because I was only playing academy football at Hampton and Richmond and my manager told me that Chertsey wanted me so I went down to training and here I am." The 2018-2019 season was his gap year "before I go to uni at Southampton". His pre-Vase final roommate Sam Flegg recalls how "Lewis told me about how much he was looking forward to going to university and I told him all about how much I missed it!"

Lewis appreciates the help Nick Jupp has given him in his 'keeper training. "Whenever we are in training or warming up he is always helping me out and giving me tips in how to improve, plus whenever I am playing he always comes down to support." Of Lewis, Kevin Maclaren wrote in the FA Vase Final programme, "Whenever he has played in the cup or league he's been very reliable and kept a few clean sheets. We're lucky to have him."

Tuesday 16th October – CC League　　　Redhill 1 Chertsey Town 4

In a game that for much of the time, the two teams matched each other, we, and in particular Jake Baxter, were far more adept at putting the ball into the net. It gave us all the points and stretched the lead in the table over the next placed side to six points with two games in hand.

Goalkeeper Nick Jupp returned to the side but Kevin Maclaren was absent from the midfield due to suspension, though inclusion was in doubt anyway due to a strain which may keep him out for a week or so. Lewis Jackson sat out on the bench for emergencies as he too was not fully fit. Dale Binns started for the first time in three games.

The two sides cancelled each other out for much of the first half with little goalmouth action going on. A half chance a piece that saw Baxter head over at one end and a routine Jupp save at the other was just about the sum of the opportunities created.

The conclusion was, come the half hour point, that it would have been a foolhardy person to have said the game would be virtually over as a contest by half time, such was the thin serving of action in each other's penalty area. But that is what happened. An electrifying ten minutes just before the break saw off our opponents, with some to spare.

Alice Graysharp with Chris Gay

The action commenced with a Sam Murphy shot that was stopped by an outstretched hand just inside the Redhill penalty area. Instead of the high to the left spot kick executed previously by Baxter, the prolific marksman fired low and to the right with enough success to put us ahead on 37 minutes. The goal triggered a flurry of activity surrounding the home 'keeper, Juan Trivino.

The Lobsters' ground sits adjacent to the main London to South Coast line but even the Brighton Belle would have difficulty in keeping up with Dale Binns on his 50-yard explosive searching sprint through the middle of the park. Keeping the ball well under control, he by-passed four men in red to swiftly enter the penalty area and released a shot that gave Trivino no chance.

That 42nd minute effort was quickly followed up just before the interval with Lubo Guentchev finishing off a low cross from the right that was put away first time from ten yards. The break could not come fast enough for the home side who might be described by then as Lobster Thermidor, such was the heat applied by our keen as mustard side that had suddenly turned up the gas.

The second half lasted just four minutes before Baxter struck again, to maintain his record of more than two goals a game with us. This time it was his head that did the damage, diverting the ball off an Andy Crossley left wing delivery. The game then slightly lost its way for fifteen minutes or more. Further goals might have been anticipated perhaps, and although one more did pop up, it came at the other end in bizarre circumstances.

One of the fun aspects of football is it unpredictability, so who would have expected the defence, which had shown such discipline in deed and formation to drop a real clanger. It was perpetrated on the hour when a back pass to Jupp lacked the required velocity. Then, with Ayokuule Odedoyin bearing down, Jupp tried to side step with the ball at his feet but was robbed in possession leaving the Redhill forward a simple tap in.

The Mighty Chertsey Town

The moment boosted the home side who put more zest into efforts to score again. They came close on a couple of occasions, culminating in a centrally placed free kick being won 20 yards from goal that failed to penetrate a crowded penalty area. But our defence remained intact for what turned into a more comfortable win on the road than the actual balance of possession might have indicated.

Saturday 20th October – CC League   Walton & Hersham 4
**   Chertsey Town 1**

It is an indication of how far we have progressed over the past few months in considering the comprehensive defeat by Walton & Hersham as a big surprise. No-one saw it coming, not even the faithful home support who had seen their side fail to win their previous six home games. The afternoon was another example of our prime nemesis getting the better of exchanges stretching well over sixty years, a series that has produced an imbalance of 77 goals to 24.

Additionally, it is becoming apparent that our players do not relish playing on artificial surfaces, or is it a mere coincidence that only one point out of six has been won so far this term in an otherwise unblemished campaign? There was every early indication that the curse of the Swans would be broken as we made a lively start, forcing a full-length Kavanagh Keadell save off Michael Peacock's second minute header from a Dale Binns free kick.

Ali Fofanah who was lively throughout for Walton, forced Nick Jupp in goal to block out a break away. This proved to be the only highlight until the 39th minute when a rash cross field pass just inside our half was intercepted. The ball was fed to Sean White who ran forward to beat the exposed Jupp. The dust hardly settled before Walton went two up. Fofanah fired in what seemed a weak 15-yard shot but the pace fooled Jupp who got down to save but the ball juggled itself over his outstretched hand and bobbled into the net.

Alice Graysharp with Chris Gay

Half time gave the chance for us to regroup, but further woe was heaped us, but not before Marlon Wallen for the hosts continued to be a handful, this time rounding his marker but firing a strong strike into the side netting. We replied with a Lubo Guentchev free kick that went a foot wide with Keadell stranded. But it was only a minute later, the 51st, when The Swans increased their already comfortable lead. Frank Ngonyaua was the man in despatching a winged cross with space to spare.

It did not take too long, another five minutes actually, for Walton to strike again. Again our defence was all awry, allowing Wallen to break through. A desperate Jupp challenge as Wallen tried to round him resulted in a spot kick which White despatched. So, four goals up with plenty of time to spare, not a unique position for a Swans versus Curfews game, looked like it could be expanded.

In fairness, we overcame that tumbling 22 minute period and at last got our game together; a qualified observation. The Walton defence might have been made to work harder in the last half hour of the game, but they stood firm and it never looked like we would make significant inroads to redress the goal imbalance.

The introduction of Dalson Ernesto and a debut for Oliver Davis looked a good move and they busily adapted well. Michael Kinsella saw a header skid wide, an Ernesto shot that went a yard wide, a looping Jake Baxter header from distance that was ruled out for offside, a Davis cross that morphed into a cunning slightly off target shot and a Guentchev shot over when receiving from an Ernesto cut back completed a list of unsuccessful half chances.

Some sort of reward was forthcoming though. It came midway through stoppage time when an Ernesto cross caught a defending arm giving Baxter the opportunity to continue his goal scoring run from the penalty spot. This he comfortably managed to do and so provide an almost respectable score line against a deserved Walton & Hersham win.

The performance in our first visit to the newly opened shared home of the Swans was not a systemic failure. Disappointing as it was, the consensus was that too many players were out of sorts. An injured, so missing, Kevin Maclaren might have had an influence but the team did well enough without his presence four days earlier, thus we have proved to be far from a one man team. No, it was just one of those days, but one that saw Chertsey Town retain their strong position at the top of the table.

Left back Mason Welch-Turner's lowest point of the season was "losing our unbeaten run in the league against Walton and Hersham who were bottom of the league and struggling. We are a team of winners and losing to a side bottom of the league was definitely not a highlight for us!"

Saturday 27th October – CC League   Chertsey Town 3 AFC Hayes 1

Following an exceptionally benign Autumn, it was a bitter wind that blew along the Alwyns Lane arena, but it was visitors AFC Hayes that felt the cold in being another Chertsey Town victim from this Combined Counties League encounter. They might wonder how they lost this game, but two simple facts and conviction highlighted the reasoning.

Conviction comes with any winning side that in keeping on plugging away will eventually win you prizes, no matter the lateness of the hour. And the facts? One was that the travellers only generated three on target or meaningful shots at goal and the other was that our back line did its job well enough to create fact number one.

Although Hayes played attractive football, being the more effective in midfield and so enjoyed greater possession, they were unable to make it count. This was not one of our better performances but we had the power to breakdown our opponent, even if for periods it looked less than likely. We always looked the more dangerous of the two sides, once the penalty areas had been breached, putting into relief that it is goals, and not just potential, that counts.

Goalkeeper Nick Jupp was first into action with a full length, but comfortable save from a low shot at range. He had two more tasks of significance during the rest of the exchange. One was to pick the ball out of his net on 37 minutes, the Hayes equaliser, and the other to hold on to a 22-yard free kick that flew straight at him in the second period. Otherwise, it was routine work all the way.

Clearances from his domain though were more direct that has been the case of late which too often resulted in possession being lost. Hayes were particularly effective at picking up the loose ball. Our normally slick close order passing also somehow deserted us, another manifestation of our opponent's superior possession time. As stated, it all came to naught for the Middlesex side, and was even exacerbated on 24 minutes when they surrendered the initiative by conceding a goal.

A midfield pass set off Andy Crossley who broke through centrally. AFC Hayes goalkeeper Cameron Kennedy blocked the goal attempt, but such was the ferocity of the strike, the ball rocketed back to Jake Baxter who, from well outside the box, let fly to find the net with Kennedy still out of position.

Given the nature of our early season matches, a thought that we might run away with the game was soon shattered. The Brook continued to look far livelier than their league position dictated. Then Adam Mohammed closed in on goal in a crowded penalty area. He was ushered to the left, but with just enough room remaining to clip the ball inside and in off the far post to deservedly redress the balance.

The Mighty Chertsey Town

Hayes always looked confident, even after the break but without a product to display. We, on the other hand, although still failing to ease into cruise control, regained the lead with a goal on 74 minutes. Crossley sent in a shot off a corner kick. The goalmouth was congested which assisted in the ball being sent away, but only to Lubo Guentchev just outside the area. He tried his luck and as the ball sped goalwards, it caught Baxter en route, enough to catch out Kennedy who got a touch to the ball but not enough to stop its progress.

The lead was very welcome but was it enough? Strong Chertsey Town marshalling at the back suggested it might be but as anything can happen in football, there was always a shadow on their ambitions. In fact most chances occurred in our favour and we should have taken better advantage. Dale Binns fired over from under the posts and Crossley made one pass too many when a shot looked favourite. However, one more goal did arrive in the game when Crossley and Kennedy clashed and a penalty kick was awarded. Baxter coolly put the ball away in the 84th minute to doubly secure the points.

Combined Counties League Premier Division
Top 4 – end of October

	P	W	D	L	F	A	Gd	Pts
Chertsey Town	12	10	1	1	29	11	*18*	31
Banstead Athletic	14	6	8	0	21	11	*10*	26
Redhill	12	7	2	3	22	14	*8*	23
Abbey Rangers	13	7	1	5	26	23	*3*	22

Saturday 3rd November – FA Vase 2nd Round   **Chertsey Town 2**
Horndean 0

Thirty-two minutes gone; Chertsey Town 0 Horndean 0. Wham, Bam, Alakazam! Thirty five minutes gone; Chertsey Town 2 Horndean 0. And so it was in those three furtive

Alice Graysharp with Chris Gay

minutes that this FA Buildbase Vase second round tie was settled with us entering the hat with 63 other hopefuls for the next stage. It was a deserved win although our Wessex League counterparts were no pushovers.

In fact the visitors finished the stronger side, playing with confidence and directness in the latter stages, but it was still insufficient to overcome our well organised and tight defence. Not being allowed to penetrate with enough menace, Horndean came closest to success at distance with Harry Jackson, in particular presenting the most danger with a late strike against the upright and another that struck the goal support, indicating the closeness of that effort.

A lesson that many of our opponents are having to endure is that if you do not take your chances against us, you will suffer the consequences. This was illustrated on 13 minutes when after a Chertsey dominated start, Horndean struck out on the counter. Swift right side movement set up Miles Everett right in front of the home goalmouth but his shot was blasted well over the cross bar.

Dale Binns made his own thrusting run ten minutes later, to create mayhem under the portals of the Horndean goal. How the ball was never forced home in the melee will never be explained. The incident signposted more Chertsey pressure though with a free kick being won after Andy Crossley was unfairly barged off the ball 20 yards from goal. Binns took the kick but the ball never threatened to make an impact, the exterior fence with Alwyns Lane aside!

We were not to be denied and by the 33rd minute we took a likely looking lead. A corner kick from the right flank was headed goalwards by Crossley. Although he was some distance out and was unlikely to find the net. Binns, right in front of goal got his head to the ball and did find the onion bag. A first thought of offside was quickly dispelled as an out of position defender was still deep enough to render such worries unfounded.

The Mighty Chertsey Town

The lead was enhanced two minutes later. A 25-yard Crossley shot engineered a corner kick on the left after goalkeeper Ross Casey made a full length save. The result was a clever routine of passes that created an angle that found the ball at the far post. It looked a mite too far but somehow Michael Peacock hooked the ball, a yard or so from the outside of the post, round the corner from only inches from the goal line and into the roof of the net.

Two up and with Jake Baxter not yet performing his regular trick of finding the net, it all looked good. Baxter worked hard to keep his record going but ultimately failed despite an 18-yard strike in the first half that was saved and plenty of invention and energy later, but it was the defence that took the limelight after the break.

It was easy to see why Horndean lie second in their league as they found reserves of commitment and enough skill to almost make a comeback. This effort increased as time leaked away for them. Wing back forays featured strongly in their game with Fuzz Kamjanda on the left prominent even if he struggled to by-pass Lewis Jackson. However, our defence remained resolute. The only concern was that if the Jackson strike had gone in and not hit the post, would the final dozen or so minutes produced an equaliser?

That was an academic question. Horndean were not alone with late goal attempts as the hard work of Lubo Guentchev was almost rewarded with a sneaky shot in a crowded area that Casey got down and saved. Although the last hour of the game yielded no further goals, the game still provided plenty of interest and a happy journey home in looking forward to the next Vase episode.

The Horndean win for Andy Crossley ranks high on his matches of the season list. "I thought the match against

Horndean at home was a huge win for us. They were a good side and it gave the boys the belief when we play well we will beat anyone."

Michael Peacock

The scorer of the second goal against Horndean, Michael Peacock joined Chertsey Town for the 2018-2019 season. "It was the third time I had signed for Dave Anderson, he's someone I have a lot of respect for and he showed real excitement at Chertsey's ambition for the season."

A centre half, Michael signed from the championship winning Beaconsfield Town and has also played for Hendon, Harrow Borough and Northwood. His shortest ever appearance in a football match was at Hendon where, "I had been ill all week before the game and started all the games prior to this; speaking to the manager he said he hoped not to use me but will keep me on the bench just in case, the team is 2-1 up with about 20 minutes to go, the manager goes to me 'Come on and make sure we don't lose', I come on, the ball gets kicked off the pitch, I run over to pick the ball up and my back goes into spasm and I can't do anything but lay down on my front. I get stretchered off after just 15 seconds and not touching the ball. Very embarrassing!"

Kevin Maclaren speaks highly of Michael in the FA Vase Final programme. "A real leader on the pitch, he wins everything in the air, heads things, kicks thing, but is very good technically, too."

Saturday 10th November – CC League **Spelthorne Sports 1**
Chertsey Town 2

We came away from rain-soaked Spelthorne Sports with a muddied 'Job Done' tag after a difficult afternoon with the narrowest of a Combined Counties League victory. The falling rain may not have suited our supporters, but it worked decisively in

The Mighty Chertsey Town

the side's performance. An early penalty bonus was tempered by the dismissal of midfielder Kevin Maclaren with almost an hour of the game still to go.

A thunderous shower of rain preceded the start of the match. This gave way to moderate but persistent rainfall that lasted into dusk. Although the super slick conditions serviced an early moment of danger for us when the ball skidded off heads to present Matthew Weston a great chance to score on three minutes, but Town goalkeeper Nick Jupp got down to the shot well, to quell the excitement.

Spelthorne were apt to pump the ball forward with overzealous gusto with the result that the ball tended to aquaplane across the well grassed surface and beyond reach. We adapted better with a shorter game but even we did not expect to take the lead after just six minutes. The ball was lobbed forward to Andy Crossley in the Sports penalty area where he was caught on the turn. Home 'keeper Hendy Poole got a touch on the Lubo Guentchev spot kick but the ball still found its mark.

Jake Baxter would normally have taken the strike but was absent with a knee injury. John Pomroy took his place for his sixth start of the season. He, in turn, was replaced at half time as target man by Dale Binns. By coincidence, the two front men have only ten weeks separating their dates of birth which raised the remarkable statistic of generating a combination of 74 years between them.

The game then progressed without trauma until an untimely high tackle by Maclaren on 33 minutes which resulted in a red card. It might have seemed harsh, given the conditions, but the iron man had already been twice warned so seemingly the referee considered he now had an expired licence. This altered the dynamic of the exchange as we were reduced to one forward.

Alice Graysharp with Chris Gay

The advantage on paper enjoyed by the Middlesex side was not translated to the sodden pitch so that our narrow advantage was still relatively comfortably retained by half time. Things were different, however, immediately after the break with Spelthorne Sports mounting an all-out assault on our lines. Although play was compressed into the last third of the battle ground, little in the way of a direct barrage was launched as our defensive structure remained tight.

The attritional effect did though produce its desired goal and an equaliser came after just five minutes of this attack. The ball just could not be cleared and it was eventually fed to the left, then returned inside where Jake Flatman hit a low penetrating strike from a dozen yards past an unsighted Jupp to even up the score, but more ominously it passed the initiative to the home side.

Spelthorne tails were thus up, but were soon lowered when a quick-fire response was conducted. Almost as a repeat performance of four minutes earlier, but with the danger emanating from the right at the other end of the park, a feed inside by Binns was only cleared as far as Dave Taylor. He took full advantage with a low penetrating strike from the edge of the penalty area that eluded Poole.

This a was a visible setback for Sports and it was not until the latter stages that they came anywhere close to pulling the game back when defender Callum MacKay cleared our cross bar from a good position, and another later effort took a similar route, but having been deflected en route that time. Prior to that little flurry, we created our own moments. Binns was the prime perpetrator with a shot that skidded 18 inches wide, and another that was scrambled away in semi panic for a corner kick.

This was no Champagne performance but will have given team boss Dave Anderson immense satisfaction in seeing his side battle through adversity with intelligent football to grab three points with a gritty display that bodes well for the deep winter months when nippy football on a pristine surface may not be the order of the day.

Tuesday 13th November – League Cup　　　　　　**Chertsey Town 3**
British Airways 2

Anyone checking up future opposition for an impending match with Chertsey Town would have been sorely disappointed, or misled. Manager Dave Anderson made seven changes to the team that started three days previous with a side that included five names that had either played for, or are currently with, the club's Under 18 squad. The occasion was the Second Round League Cup tie with Combined Counties Division One side British Airways.

The playing conditions here were perfect. Pitch and weather combined to encourage the best football possible. The changed line up introduced an air of uncertainty with only first choice Mason Welch-Turner, Kevin Maclaren, Danny Bennell, John Pomroy and Dale Binns featuring at the start. With five teenagers included, mainly at 17 years, the age profile dropped dramatically from the norm despite four of the other starters being in their thirties.

It was, therefore, a blend of exuberant youth and old stager experience that was enough to overcome the opposition, even if the result made the game as close as the final score line suggests. It was as well an early two goal lead was banked in what seemed to be a regulation and undramatic win for us, developed into a tightly contested tie.

It was the failure of the Bluebirds to tuck away their chances that made the difference. Although we had the edge in control, the Division One side showed up well and was a credit to Step Six football. The miss of the game was perpetrated by their number 11, Jeff Kalejaye, when he took three touches when

Alice Graysharp with Chris Gay

one, a thump into the net from eight yards, looked favourite. Avoiding that error midway through the second half would have made it anyone's tie.

Early success came when Arlie Talboys, one of the Under 18s players, set up John Pomroy. He triggered a strong shot which was blocked by Nathan Dyos in goal. Unfortunately for him, the ball rebounded in Oliver Davis' direction and he fired home from ten yards to create a fifth minute lead for our side.

It was not long before goal number two arrived. Davis again featured, but this time by being clipped from behind, even though he was facing away from goal, but inside the penalty area. Dale Binns took the spot kick which smashed into the back of the net despite Dyos getting a touch. It looked all plain sailing as a third almost came before the break when the speed of Mason Welch-Turner, when roaring along the left flank, brought him into close proximity of goal but he eventually ran out of space.

The game did see a third goal before halftime; on 44 minutes to be precise. It came as a shock after noting little in the way of British Airways enterprise in front of our goal, but this on occasion saw Jake Morten make advantage of a slight deflection and slot the ball home off Lewis Gallifent's left stick.

Although Kalejaye may make that subsequent horror and potentially equalising miss, he did well just after the resumption to create an initial equaliser by turning on the ball and directing it well clear of Gallifent from a dozen yards. The equal status of the game lasted but six minutes before we regained the lead, not to be relinquished for the remaining 35 minutes.

It was a trade-mark John Pomroy effort in sliding in on the far post to connect with a left wing diagonal cross that hardly left the ground in its projection. The Middlesex side tried their best to come back but were denied. Apart from the miss, a key Talboys tackle late in the game kept our opponents firmly on

Danny Bennell

Featuring in the starting line up in this League Cup tie, having joined Chertsey Town late in the 2017-2018 season, 35 year old central defender Danny brought many years of experience to his game including playing in an FA Vase Final for Hillingdon Borough. He had also been with North Greenford United and Hanwell Town. "When Dave Anderson was appointed," says Danny, "his assistant Steve Hawkins, my first senior, called and sold me the season's dream but told me if they didn't first achieve survival the dream would've been dead in the water."

Unfortunately for Danny, while he was on the beach on August Bank Holiday, "I tore my meniscus, played the following game against Woodley in the Vase through pain, missed five to six weeks after that in which I lost my place. But in a team who keeps winning and wanting to improve I had no problem with it." Jake Baxter confirms Danny's generous attitude. "Danny turns up to every training session, gives 100% in everything we do, never moans if he doesn't get picked, he just turns round and supports the people who have been picked in front of him. He'd be involved in every social get together and I don't think anyone would have a bad word to say about him."

Saturday 17th November – CC League   **Chertsey Town 3**
Banstead Athletic 3

We could not work out whether we should have laughed or cried over our Combined Counties League encounter with visitors Banstead Athletic. We were certainly crying at half time in seeing the side three goals down, but laughing at full time after a remarkable second half recovery that bought the scores level. In analysis, the laughter out shrieked the tears, for it eventually felt more like a win than a draw.

Banstead Athletic arrived with eleven of their 16-man squad having played for us within the past 12 months. Despite any rivalry, the game was played in a good, but competitive heart and it was the generous helpings of ball in the back of the net incidences that took centre stage of this highly entertaining exchange. Six goals were permitted but one, thought to be the opener, was denied in the most bizarre circumstances.

A short pass free kick awarded to us on the left flank set up a perfect angle for Andy Crossley to float in a shot that flew well clear of all players, including Fraser Tugwell in the Banstead goal. Despite the loftiness of the ball that dropped into the far side top corner of the net and a lack of anyone attempting to address the ball, the referee acceded to the linesman's offside flag, prompting wonderment by everyone, amber or blue, how someone 40 yards away and at right angles to the action could have deduced that there was interference in those circumstances.

Frustration was compounded nine minutes later when, on 25 minutes, we found ourselves one goal down instead of one up! It has to be said the goal was not undeserved for the Banstead Athletic side acted as one in harassing and out muscling our more measured approach. Shutting down and playing with turbo powered energy paid dividends. The opening goal came from a left wing cross that Tommy Batten headed firmly home at our back stick.

As if to prove this was no fluke, a mirror image goal fired Athletic into a two goal lead just four minutes later. This time it was an angled free kick on the right, again to the back post where, again, Batten rushed in unchallenged to firmly head home. We were fortunate not to go three down on 35 minutes

The Mighty Chertsey Town

when the ball flashed across our goalmouth, but no-one managed a connection when a touch was all that was required.

The third did come though, just a minute or two before the interval when home thoughts were forlornly resting on the fantasy that a goal pulled back before the break would then open up the game once more. That notion never looked reality in the face for we rarely looked like finding the net (again!) at that stage.

In fact, more misery was generated after Mason Welch-Turner was dispossessed midway in the Banstead Athletic half with us on the attack. The ball was swiftly sent up field in one raking motion to Tommy Hutchins who ran on through a sparse Town defence and thumped the ball home in delightful style. Well, that should have been that! The three goal, not so much a cushion, but more a mattress, should have been perfectly adequate to see the away side through to the win. But football always manages to surprise.

Even so, the 'surprise' still did not look on, come the hour mark being passed. We had quelled the Banstead onslaught but it still seemed the status quo would be maintained, even if maybe one goal might have been conjured to make the score line look a bit more respectable. That was until the 65th minute when a rash challenge through the calves of Crossley on the extremities of the Banstead penalty area was perpetrated.

The spot kick was put away, low this time, by Jake Baxter to provide the spark for a remarkable Chertsey revival. The comeback kids suddenly found the key to the crock of goal! Heavy pressure was mounted and a reward arrived only three minutes later. A throw came in from the right where the ball was squared inside to the edge of the Banstead box. Although there were plenty of shirts on station, debut boy Johan Becka, who had replaced Connor Maclaren only minutes previously, somehow found the target through the forest of legs.

Alice Graysharp with Chris Gay

The shot was not particularly convincing but it had direction on its side by clipping the right post, then to dribble across the line and nestle in the far side netting. A goal is a goal though, and this one added to the game's grandstand finale. The physical edge of Banstead Athletic understandably subsided, possibly through events plus an inability to maintain their high tractive effort in any event. Certainly the spearheading Hutchins on pain killers in the Banstead attack was suffering as the tables turned, but not completely, in the hosts' favour.

But it looked a good chance that we might equalise, and so it came to pass. It came on 83 minutes, but initially at that moment looked as if the opportunity had passed. A goalmouth melee was somehow repressed but the let up lasted less than ten seconds for back came the ball to the six-yard area. This time a blue and white man, in fact Michael Kinsella, won the frantic battle, to knock the ball over the line in untidy fashion.

The game was not done yet. We continued to press and a fourth was not beyond the realms of fantasy this time, however, it looked like it was going to be our visitors' day when the ball was headed towards the Chertsey net in stoppage time with goalkeeper Nick Jupp well beaten. From almost nowhere though, Welch-Turner saved the day by rushing in and with contorted neck action, headed the ball away to safety to keep scores level.

It was ironic that the best goal of the game did not count. Banstead Athletic certainly scored their three in style; ours were ugly. In the whole scheme of things though, the seven, net six, all contributed, with the players' efforts of course, to create what might be regarded as one of the more memorable afternoons of the season at Alwyns Lane.

For some of the Chertsey players, Banstead at home was (apart from the Championship win at Hayes and the Wembley

Final) one of their top choice matches of the season. Michael Peacock explains.

"A real stand out game for me was the 3-3 draw with Banstead, there was a bit of needle in the game as it was the ex-Chertsey manager bringing his new team, I was actually injured and Kevin Maclaren also missed the game, so missing two leaders of the team we found ourselves 3-0 down at half time. To come back and draw the game 3-3 showed how much character this team has, and just one example of the team's never say die attitude."

When I asked Dave Anderson for a resumé of his Banstead at home half time team talk he said it was unprintable. Jake Baxter recalls, "Dave had a massive go at us half time, the only time I can remember this happening to us, then Kevin spoke to the team just before we went out and said we owe Dave a massive performance second half. We came out, got the three goals and should have won it late on but I felt that proved to everyone what we was about and showed the togetherness of the squad on what was our first tricky game."

The game had special significance too for Michael Kinsella. "After a tough half time team talk and looking at ourselves in the mirror we came back and drew 3-3 – I got the equaliser. We never knew when we were beat. From then on we felt nobody could beat us."

Tuesday 20th November – Surrey Senior Cup   Walton & Hersham 2
Chertsey Town 2

(Chertsey Town win 5-3 on penalties)

In almost a reverse situation of three days previous, we took a seemingly comfortable two goal lead after just 16 minutes to put us into cruise control but in the end we were mightily pleased to have reached the end of open play on terms with hosts Walton & Hersham in a rain soaked Surrey Senior Cup tie.

Alice Graysharp with Chris Gay

Neither side fielded their strongest side. That statement might be presumptive because Swans' manager, Dickson Gill had resigned the previous day so who knows what disruption that created in the Walton camp? In the event, that side did well to hold together a more than creditable show.

Our line-up was not all that dissimilar to that played seven days earlier against British Airways. They made a bright start which was made brighter with only seven minutes when a fantastic flighted 50-yard diagonal cross from Arlie Talboys was ably collected by Lubo Guentchev. He took the ball on and dropped it over the head of a defenceless Kavanagh Keadell in the Walton goal.

It got better for us seven minutes later with a through ball threaded to John Pomroy who fired home low across the face of goal from 20 yards. Walton were unlucky soon after when Monty Everett forced a way through our defence but then hit the post with his shot.

Both sides were prone to giving away free kicks in dangerous areas but none were made to count. Lewis Gallifent took the position between the sticks and played a major part in keeping us in the game commencing with a brave block after Everett had broken through.

It was about this time, a third way through the tie that the home side started to take the initiative. It could be said that the final 60 minutes was not our finest hour. Our usual slick passing deserted us, clearances from defence were continually collected by a Walton man and too often we tried to force open passages that just were not there.

However, the half time break arrived and our defences were still intact but it did not take long after the start of the second half for that thought to become just a recent memory. A fierce inch perfect shot from just inside the box rattled our cage as it hit the back of the net eight minutes into the turnaround.

The Mighty Chertsey Town

Gallifent had no chance with that one but he did exceedingly well with other efforts which was just as well as there was only one side in the chase for a place in Round Two despite Andy Crossley joining in off the bench to pep up our attack.

It was midfield play though that lacked enough guile to relative pressure at the back, pressure that gave way again on 82 minutes when, from a corner kick created after yet another acrobatic Gallifent save that saw the ball pushed aside. From the kick, it came to just outside our penalty area. A Walton player on station there, pulled the trigger and was rather fortunate to see his effort take two deflections on its way to recording the equaliser.

It was only then we created some sustained danger for the first time in the second half but both sides held out to the final whistle and instantly into the penalty shoot-out, now that extra time is abolished in this competition.

We started the sequence through Guentchev and ran in all five efforts thanks also to Crossley, Pomroy, Dave Taylor and Mason Welch-Turner. Walton missed their first attempt and although the following two were successful, we were too far ahead for a home side fifth attempt. It was a bit of a get out of jail card being played but nonetheless, it got us through to a January date in this competition.

Chertsey Town winning 5-3 on penalties. The shape of things to come…?

From The Secretary's Quill November

Me aside (!), we have had some bright luminaries down here at Alwyns Lane over the years. Most have related to the football world of course, both on and off the field of play (Kenny Sansom for instance, or Mick McCarthy) but some have been from other spheres (Russell Grant, Alan Simpson, Runnymede Borough Mayors). We have even had an amalgam of these two diverse worlds when actor Ralf Little donned our stripes for competitive matches.

With all respect to these personalities, I think we hit the peak last week on the football side of things when the actual chairman of the Football Association, Greg Clarke, arrived on a busman's holiday excursion for our game with Banstead Athletic. He came over as a most personable sort of bloke with no airs or graces and, I believe, with a genuine desire to appreciate how football ticks at our level. I wish I knew!

Why did he come here? First of all, he lives locally; not actually Chertsey, but only a couple of miles away. There was no top rank domestic football on offer due to the internationals weekend. Plus, Alwyns Lane is hardly doom and gloom valley at present.

His response to his afternoon with us was, "I'm loving it!" I think it was more the entertainment of the actual match that prompted the remark, but he did also give a genuine air of enjoying his off duty afternoon. I wonder if he will come again? He knows we might be able to fit him in!

Saturday 24th November – CC League   **Chertsey Town 2**
                                            Guildford City 2

Our home league match with Guildford City put us on the back foot for much of the game and in the end we had to be satisfied with a draw against one of the best displays put up against us so far this season. We dropped behind twice but each time fought back each time. If nothing else, manager Dave Anderson will be pleased with the side's resilience, even if a victory was not achieved.

City began in smart fashion and Nick Jupp was forced into an early significant save off the head of Nemo Adams. But

The Mighty Chertsey Town

three minutes later, on ten minutes, Guildford did find the net, rather fortuitously from the penalty spot when a rough bounce caught an arm in the area allowing Benga Ogunseye to fire low past Jupp.

It took only six minutes for the equaliser to arrive when goalkeeper Oneal Garnes failed to hold a strike and Lubo Guentchev collected the ball and hit home the rebound. A scare for us when Jupp handled what was adjudged a back pass, some 15 yards from goal. The moment quickly passed as City were unable to force the ball through a packed defence. Both sides had chances in an open game but the score remained in balance at the interval.

More opportunities were created immediately after the break with Benga Ogunseye firing straight at Jupp at one end and a ball headed back across a gaping goalmouth, but without anyone making a connection, at the other. It was still nip and tuck.

More chances went each way but it was Guildford City that took theirs first. This time it was Eli Ogunseye on the score sheet after finishing off a neat move by heading in a cross to the near post. The 76th minute goal might have finished the resolve of many sides but we have shown reserves of mental strength this term, especially in the latter stages of games and we came back to snatch the draw with the confident City slickers.

This resilience was rewarded on 82 minutes with Guentchev again hitting the Guildford City net when finding space enough to calmly lob the ball over Garnes. There was still plenty of forward action from both sides in the final flurry but each side had to settle for a point a piece.

Alice Graysharp with Chris Gay

Combined Counties League Premier Division
Top 4 End of November

	P	W	D	L	F	A	Gd	Pts
Chertsey Town	15	11	3	1	36	17	19	36
Banstead Athletic	15	10	2	3	29	17	12	32
Redhill	16	10	1	5	33	26	7	31
Abbey Rangers	17	10	1	6	30	29	1	31

Saturday 8th December – FA Vase 3rd Round   **Redbridge 0**
Chertsey Town 5

Never were the effects of Murphy's Law, the one that says if anything can go wrong, it will, further from our minds when visiting the borders of Essex and East London for the delayed FA Vase tie. Why? Because number ten, Sam Murphy could do no wrong for he fired home a hattrick of goals as we cruised into the last 32 of the competition at the expense of hosts Redbridge.

It had been some time since manager Dave Anderson had been able to field his strongest side. Three previous successive 90-minute draws was an amber light, perhaps, that our troops were losing that winning habit. This emphatic victory over mid table Essex Senior League opposition put that vague theory to rest as we poetically returned to our best, whist still maintaining a healthy lead at the top of the Combined Counties League after a fortnight's leave of absence from that stage.

On an only just, playable pitch after prolonged rain, it took a while to assert our will but once the first goal was recorded it was Surrey all the way. Aided by poor clearances in the opening gambit, Redbridge had the greater share of possession. It took a good quarter of an hour's play though before any real pressure was exerted on our penalty area. The Motormen's attack flattered to deceive with promising approach work that then generally came to nothing with Chertsey ramparts remaining intact.

The Mighty Chertsey Town

This situation morphed into action at the other end. A short corner on the left created an angle for Lubo Guentchev to launch the missile into the face of the goal. In an almost impossible to defend situation, Sam Murphy flashed the ball into the back of the net for a 23rd minute lead; one that never looked like being dissolved from then on.

The goal put extra fizz into the attack. The home side's goalkeeper was Chico Ramos, a considerable frame that had donned Chertsey Town colours 21 times over the previous two seasons. He kept an eager Chertsey attack at bay, as best he could. His efforts, coupled with a less than firm surface in that territory, combined to keep us out with either a series of full length saves or weakened shots, dampened in not being able to get purchase on an unstable launch pad.

Dale Binns made telling runs on the left and fired off a powerful shot that Ramos parried. Murphy, Baxter and Crossley all had scoring ambitions around a particularly vibrant spell on the half hour. But the Essex defence could not prevail when, on 38 minutes, Murphy struck again. His goal followed the only chance of the first half for the home side to make an impression when number eleven, Sam Phillips, fired a corner kick over the bar when under pressure.

Back at other end; possession was gained when Redbridge were attempting to ease away from goal, wide on their left. The ball was snatched away by Guentchev and quickly knocked inside where Murphy had room to advance and direct the ball to the side, a well-placed effort from 15 yards that opened up a two-goal gap that was maintained at the interval.

Home thoughts of repairing first half damage were dispelled early on when goal number three arrived on 53 minutes. Binns won possession, then threaded a delightful pass through the retreating defenders to Murphy who struck again with a well-aimed delivery from near the penalty spot. If thoughts of a home revival were unrealistically still prevailing up to that point they were then well and truly despatched.

In fairness, the Motormen continued to make a contest of it but the fuel dial was showing red as we asserted near full control. Our defence, and midfield, were continually nicking the ball off the limited Redbridge men. With Murphy now with a hattrick tucked under his belt, it was time for a more likely marksman to get in on the act. A ball delivered over an overstretched home defence was meat and drink to Jake Baxter. He collected the ball, still in a deep position, and then exploited a gaping hole past Ramos from well outside the box for number four, come 66 minutes.

The fifth exploded on the scene on 74 minutes. It was Binns again who picked up on a loose ball. This time he took it forward himself on an extended run and nearly broke the net with a 15-yard blast. This then allowed a reshuffle from the bench with John Pomroy, Connor Maclaren and Dave Taylor on to replace Binns, Baxter and Guentchev, who all made full contributions.

A forlorn reply was attempted late on when Patrick Duggen fired forcefully, straight into the arms of Nick Jupp in goal as the game came gently to a conclusion, when even full back Mason Welch-Turner was allowed to foray forward to find himself in the heart of the attack at one time. Although five goals suggested the attack, and in particular Sam Murphy, might take all the accolades, this has to be considered as an all-round performance with the midfield and defence playing a full part, especially in the early stages when Redbridge looked a useful outfit.

In the coach getting the side to all sing from the same hymn sheet, it was a job well done with no down sides, other than to give the Chertsey laundry department a real job in cleaning off the Essex mud from the all yellow kit!

The Mighty Chertsey Town

Sam Murphy

Match ball winner of the FA Vase tie away to Redbridge, midfielder Sam Murphy joined Chertsey Town in the close season of 2018 from Hendon for whom he had played 184 matches. He was previously at Edgware Town and Aldershot Town, having started his footballing career as part of Cambridge United's Academy. "I joined Chertsey at the beginning of the season when Kevin Maclaren who is a good mate of mine told me he was setting up a team with Dave Anderson. I've known and played with Kev for years and had numerous battles against Dave when I was at Hendon and he was at Harrow, so I knew something good was about to happen when they both joined forces. Stepping into the changing room on the first day I knew quite a few of the boys. Instantly I knew we would do great things because not only were the likes of Binnsy, Peacock, Lubo all great players, they were top people and would all add to the dressing room environment."

Normally a provider rather than a goal poacher, his hattrick in the game against Redbridge doubled Sam's goals total for Chertsey in all competitions and he went on to further exhibit his goalscoring talent in the very next league match. In the FA Vase Final programme Kevin Maclaren describes Sam as "a technical footballer who has the quality to find the killer pass. He will cover more grass than anyone else."

Saturday 15th December – CC League   **Chertsey Town 6**
Walton & Hersham 0

A match against Walton & Hersham has usually signalled disaster for us in the past but on this occasion, the boot was well and truly on the other foot in our home Combined Counties League encounter. The six goal margin actually flattered the Swans who were swept aside by a rampant Curfew side. Striker Jake Baxter may have hit another hattrick, his third in nine outings for us, but it was the surging left flank runs by Dale Binns that warmed home support on a very wet and raw afternoon.

The two sides had recently met in cup and league exchanges when we had struggled, but from the off, the perception was that this contest was going in quite a different direction. Michael Peacock in central defence was unavailable but, on debut, Quincy Rowe fitted in as if he had been in situ all season. Goalkeeper Nick Jupp was also absent but young Lewis Gallifent again comfortably filled that role, even if he needs to improve his kicking skills.

It took only six minutes of play, mainly in one direction, before we took the lead. Advancement to the goal was near perfection with defender Mason Welch-Turner feeding Andy Crossley on the left. His far post cross found Lubo Guentchev who headed the ball back inside for Baxter to sweep it into the net. Pat Kirby came closest to potentially putting the brakes on the runaway Chertsey train with a 25-yard free kick that curled away from Gallifent but then struck the outside of the upright and away to safety.

Guentchev had a couple of excellent opportunities to record goals but it was not to be his day. The first of these came on the quarter hour mark when he fired directly at the busy Kavanagh Keadell in goal after more attractive approach work. He was unlucky ten minutes later in directing the ball wide from a good position after a devastating Binns run on the left had ripped open the Walton defence.

Another forging Binns run via the same route teased Keadell out of his goal and well out of position. The veteran attacker was just too quick for the 'keeper in clipping the ball to the centre for Sam Murphy to fire into the inviting net. It could, or maybe should, have been three on 34 minutes when Guentchev was put away with only one man to beat. The crowd urged him to put his boot through the leather but a moment of hesitation

The Mighty Chertsey Town

resulted in recovery by our visitors' defence and the moment was lost.

A three-goal gap was established though by half time. It was that man Binns again. He beat two attendees on entering the Walton box and along the goal line, when tripped as he attempted to accelerate away. An inevitable penalty kick was awarded which was comfortably tucked away by striker Baxter for an even more comfortable interval lead.

The relentless rain increased in intensity after the break, to be matched by our play, possibly the best home performance for many years, but not before an early Kirby strike went narrowly wide for Walton. Any chance of the sort of revival, as seen in November at Alwyns Lane when a three-goal interval lead was nullified, was killed off after 11 minutes of action. Welch-Turner again set an attack in motion with a through ball to Baxter who ran on and steered his third past Kavanagh.

Now with four goals to play with, substitutions were enacted beginning with the introduction of Fred Hill, newly arrived from Redhill, who replaced the exalted Dale Binns with his job well done. Hill showed to be a lively attacker despite the increasingly slick conditions, by frequently supplying the ball into the Walton penalty area from wide positions. The visitors' number two Luke Randall had a torrid time with Binns and if he thought that his withdrawal would make life easier then he soon saw the error of his ways!

Most of our forward production continued on the left as Welch-Turner again progressed the ball forward, this time to Murphy whose end product, after carving through all before him, was a side footed shot that skidded just wide. Walton tried their best to reply but our defence always seemed to have an extra man and the opposition's attack invariably needed to beat two men to make progress; a forlorn quest. The adjectives, 'organised' and 'comprehensive' did not do justice to the defending.

The attack took the limelight toward the game's conclusion. Walton were getting battered and so no surprise was experienced when the fifth goal arrived. It was Connor Maclaren, on for Guentchev in the 71st minute, who smashed the ball across the Walton goal face from 20 yards on 75 minutes. The goal emanated, for a change, from the right side but normal left side service was resumed ten minutes later when the ball broke from the midfield for Hill to hone in on goal.

He had his chance to score after just 19 minutes on the track but instead unselfishly nicked the ball to Murphy who was able to pick his spot from ten yards with the Swans defence again shredded. No let-up was afforded in the final few minutes with us continuing to dissect the Walton back line. Hill missed an absolute sitter and Dave Taylor, another from the bench, hit the wrong side of the side netting. These moments let off Walton having to suffer the same seven goal defeat they inflicted on us last term, but no-one was complaining.

Quincy Rowe

Chertsey Town's home game against Walton & Hersham in the league saw Quincy Rowe's debut. Having played for Staines Town, AFC Wimbledon, Harrow Borough and, most recently, Tooting & Mitcham, by the late autumn of 2018 attacking midfielder Quincy Rowe had reached 30 and was considering retirement when the opportunity arose instead to sign for Chertsey Town. This proved to be an invaluable decision for Chertsey especially when the central defence was depleted by Michael Kinsella's injury where Quincy slotted in well, providing both a defensive and, on occasion, an attacking role. This win at home to Walton & Hersham was for Quincy one of his top choice games of the season. "I'd not played for a month and I was really focused on playing well and it was great to be out there and I felt I had a really good game."

The Mighty Chertsey Town

Chris Gay has his own reason for rating this game in his top three. "The club [Walton & Hersham] has been Chertsey Town's nemesis over decades, always beating us and always at least one league level above us. Not now!"

AUTUMN 2018

Lubomir Guentchev

Back of the net!

Connor Maclaren

Lewis Gallifent with Young Player of the Year Award

Alice Graysharp with Chris Gay

Michael Peacock

Danny Bennell

The Mighty Chertsey Town

Sam Murphy chasing the ball at West Auckland

Quincy Rowe outjumping the Southall opposition

WINTER 2018/19

Saturday 22nd December – CC League   Balham 1 Chertsey Town 2

As a spectacle, it would not have been surprising if, at half time, a policeman came sauntering along with the standard phrase, "move along people, there's nothing to see!" Although there was plenty of endeavour, no wow factor lifted the first half of our League visit to Balham's Kingston-By-Pass home. It was not a featureless affair but there were few highlights.

Amongst others, two seemingly undramatic and perhaps over-zealous cautions, one to each side, were issued by the referee to control an unremarkable contest in terms of sportsmanship. The act turned into major event later when the respective players earned, creditable this time, yellow cards and were thus each dismissed in entirely separate incidents. Seven flashes of yellow were seen in a routine sort of match which made one wonder what dramas were being observed by the man in the middle, but missed by everyone else!

Back to the actual football; a somewhat middle paced opening 20 minutes produced benign probes at either end but then an injection of energy suddenly sparked the attack with a corner kick and a narrowly off target Michael Peacock shot in result. Another moment came when it looked likely that the ball would settle in the Balham net before a goalmouth melee was cleared.

We showed more invention in going forward whilst Balham were wont to punt the ball forward, more in hope than expectation, as the game again moulded back into an attritional shroud. The home side were well organised in defence and allowed little scope for any Chertsey incursions but a lapse did occur as half time approached when a weak back pass let in Jake Baxter, but his snap shot at goal was blocked by goalkeeper Kam Blonski on the edge of his area.

Baxter is almost a perpetual motion machine. This trait manufactured our first goal just after the turnaround. Not for the first, or last time in the exchange, he hustled and bustled at

The Mighty Chertsey Town

close quarters and on this occasion induced a shove in the back from his marker about the nether regions of the Balham penalty area. Having created the situation, it was only right that same striker took the spot kick and, as usual, executed the task by giving the 'keeper no chance.

Soon after, a clever Andy Crossley cross from the right when sliding along the floor encouraged an even cleverer volley from Sam Murphy, but the ball cleared bar and post, but only by inches. A brief surrender of territory soon gave way to seeing us back on the attack. Balham had a difficult enough task of getting an equaliser with eleven men on the park; they had not managed a shot, let alone one on target. Matters were made even harder for them in the 74th minute.

If Balham's Anthony Thompson was unlucky to be booked in the first half, it was a more justifiable yellow that dismissed him from the arena, received when he blocked off a surging Dale Binns break. Three minutes later it looked all up for The Blazers when Baxter again was in the vanguard. A seemingly safe situation as the home defence began to work the ball up field was disrupted with our prime striker rushing in to block the intended outward pass.

The ball ballooned up in the air. Baxter reacted first to claim possession, move forward 15 or so yards, then fire past the exposed Blonski. The two-goal cushion, created on 77 minutes, looked comfortable enough as we engaged cruise control with Balham still thwarted from putting in a shot at goal. The warm glow of a job well done turned into an uninviting chill just about on the 90-minute mark when a free kick was conceded almost 30 from goal.

It was at this point that the yellow, then red card was shown to Quincy Rowe for kicking the ball away. Probably because of the distraction that caused, and perhaps a lack of concentration, but an opening was afforded as Hamish Frew opted for a direct shot which flew past Lewis Gallifent into the net. The gap now closed, the home team went into overdrive in the remainder of stoppage time and produced more menace in those few minutes than the rest of the game combined.

It was all to no avail though for although the ball was pumped into our penalty area, with its potential consequences, the defence held firm even if it caused a few heart flutters, ones that really did not seem likely to occur, even five minutes previous. With the travelling fans desperate to hear the twitterings of a corpulent female, they were just as happy to accept one of the same; the welcome last blast of the referee's well worked whistle for the afternoon.

Life as a Chertsey Town footballer isn't just about football. The Christmas season is a time of socialising, friends and family finding time to get together and workmates organising works and office parties. The Chertsey Town footballers were no different. Danny Bennell takes up the story. "We went out for a team get together at Christmas. In the early hours of the morning I borrowed a player's phone to call home. The following Wednesday he must've been chasing up a lady he met and noticed a random number. Thinking it was this lady, he asked her out for a drink, smooth talking her – not realising it was my wife as he'd forgotten I'd borrowed his phone!"

December drew to a close in style with a 5-1 win over Knaphill on 29th December. Jake Baxter netted four goals and Binns the fifth.

The Mighty Chertsey Town

Combined Counties League Premier Division
Top 4 places at the end of December

	P	W	D	L	F	A	Gd	Pts
Chertsey Town	18	14	3	1	49	19	30	45
Banstead Athletic	20	14	3	3	40	21	19	45
Redhill	24	9	11	4	38	28	10	38
Abbey Rangers	20	10	4	6	40	35	5	34

Saturday 5th January – FA Vase 4th Round   Chertsey Town 5 St Austell 0
Our impressive FA Vase run was extended with this compressive win over Cornish visitors, AFC St Austell. Although it became a runaway victory, things could have been so different had Nick Jupp in goal had not been so agile. He was involved in two major moments during the initial stages that could have turned the match, but was the winner each time.

The first came with a planted cross from the right. Jupp went to collect a split second before Liam Eddy who nudged the goalkeeper's forearm to get a toe to the spiller ball which trundled into the net; goal disallowed! That moment came on 16 minutes. Eight minutes later, a St Austell break saw the same forward make excellent progress to a point that seemed inevitable success would follow, but a reaction save from Eddy's fierce shot using the same forearm literally saved the day. Our defences were otherwise rarely breached as another tight rear guard laid more foundation stones for victory.

The away side may have lamented those potentially tie winning moments but we too had early opportunities. A well struck Sam Murphy effort from 25 yards on just five minutes went narrowly wide. This was quickly followed by Lubo Guentchev skewing wide from a promising position. The 27th minute saw Dale Binns in the action with a shot that was parried by the busy Jason Chapman in the visitors' goal. The ball returned to Binns, but this time he fired the return over the bar.

Murphy had another go at goal by latching on to a defence splitting through ball, but Will Tinsley recovered and got a toe to the slightly delayed shot. Although we had to be patient, it felt like a goal was on its way. The prediction bore fruit on 33 minutes. Seeing Binns make a run on the right flank for a change confused spectators, so what must it have done to his adversaries? In typical fashion, he got close to the goal line, cut the ball back inside, then watched Jake Baxter put it away.

That goal was followed five minutes later, the 38th, with another Baxter strike. The St Austell defence, although under pressure, generally kept good station, but not this time. Andy Crossley and Sam Murphy together shut down a release of ball up field and got it to a very unmarked Baxter on the edge of the area where he was able to pick his spot and choose which part of the net to bulge!

A two goal interval lead was very handy but it could well have been three. A Murphy run fed Binns whose subsequent shot was blocked. The ball spilled back to the supplier but his effort went wide. So far so good.

Guentchev was the first to create the chance to open the gap further and thus to thwart any sign of a Cornish revival. However, his shot across the goalmouth went a smidge wide, having already beaten Chapman.

The back of the St Austell resistance was broken on 59 minutes with Baxter notching a third hattrick in his last four outings. Guentchev then got his goal, on 71 minutes. Persistent pressure by Kevin Maclaren found a crowded path to the edge of the penalty area from where he delivered a shot at goal. Not for the first time, the ball was not held. It fell back to the temporary striker, now to the side of goal, from where he passed it inside for an easy conversion and goal number four.

The Mighty Chertsey Town

Three minutes later, it was 5-0. Murphy, later named as man of the match, at last got his name on the score sheet after Binns created a hole for him to run through and bypass Chapman. A consolation goal might have been recorded late on when Mark Goldsworthy was allowed a free header from a cross from right, a rare Chertsey defensive lapse, but the bell had already tolled for the visitors who, although had first half issues with an otherwise excellent piece of refereeing, acknowledged that the game rightly got away from them.

The St Austell game was a good example of the extra boost provided by team spirit. "I really enjoyed the St Austell game at home," says Sam Murphy, "because I got the feeling that they fancied themselves. This got our backs up and we were all massively pumped up in the changing room. Dave Anderson then bowls in and is fuming because they have put their team's flag right next to our dugout. He gave a brilliant team talk that day and we came flying out the blocks beating them 5-0 in front of our home fans. After that vase win, that's when people started to believe. Our team was gelling and people were performing immensely week in week out."

From the Secretary's January Quill

Meeting Cornwall again revives my memories of a Vase adventure from that neck of the woods. It was a fifth round tie against Falmouth Town played in February 1988.

Home supporters will know that our pitch drains exceedingly well. However, there is a tendency in exceptionally wet spells when the River Thames is in full flow, to back up water which forces the adjacent River Bourne to flood designated areas in relief. One of those areas is half of our pitch!

And so it came to pass. Sustained rain did fall leading up to the home Falmouth match. To be played on a Saturday, there was still a foot of water lying on the far side on the Wednesday, but the tide was receding and standing water had all but gone by the Thursday. There was though some residue to wheel barrow away.

Travel was not so slick in those days so two overnight stops were involved, and with no prize fund or other FA financial support, you might imagine the stress generated by both clubs. Could the game be staged? We were grateful when former Chairman (who will be here today) Tony Gibbon donated a lorry load of sand. This was spread and the pitch hand rolled over a laid tarpaulin sheet. Hardly ideal but it did a job.

The Falmouth manager was not impressed. A former Met policeman, he had a sharp personality to match and everything he could in playing mind games. The match was staged but produced no goals even after extra time. The pitch was wrecked!

The replay was just as fraught. We set off on the Friday; mid-afternoon and arrived around nine in the evening. All was well until entering Falmouth when rain began to fall. It did not stop until the following afternoon. The referee, who came from Portsmouth, was doubtful on the Saturday morning that the game should be played but, with a bit of iffy logic about weather prospects and the playing surface, was persuaded otherwise. The cost of a postponement would have spelt disaster.

We would not have played in normal circumstances but these were special times and his decision to give it a go was justified. The danger was that if the game was abandoned, the pitch might be too damaged to try again on the Sunday, Plan B. The game went ahead, again with their manager up to his tricks (having the dressing room floor doused in water and ensuring no pre-match tea, a requirement in those days, was provided).

So the game was played and we won. Their pitch was also wrecked, and we had a great time touring Falmouth's drinking

The Mighty Chertsey Town

> dens that night. The sun shone on the Sunday which just about summed up the whole adventure. My wife will hopefully not read this story so I can say, for all sorts of reasons (but nothing dodgy I might add), it was the most memorable weekend of my life. One that ended on a fantastic high and epitomised the spirit engendered by being involved with the FA Vase.

Tuesday 8th January – Surrey Senior Cup   Chertsey Town 1
**   Sutton United 0**

Both teams avoided playing their premium sides in this Surrey Senior Cup tie but the quality of football was still high by Alwyns Lane standards. We made big changes from our Vase win of three days previous with only four starters from that game kicking off against Sutton. Our visitors featured only two first team players but the National League club demonstrated their depth of squad with a strong, but young line up.

The first half hour, or more, saw us defending in depth. Sutton entered our penalty area on numerous occasions but were not allowed a clear-cut chance. The Curfews' defence was sound and organised and protected goalkeeper Lewis Gallifent well, but even he dealt competently with all that came his way. Although the last third of the park was mainly controlled by United, they just could not find a way through and any shot that was delivered was either off target or too weak to threaten.

This was all well and good as far as we were concerned, but it was not the way to win games. Patience prevailed however, and gradually us as the home side began to break out. Ineffective as it may have been, the first 'blue shoots' sprung from the encounter with a speculative lob effort at distance from Lubo Guentchev but his attempt did not have the legs to overcome Christian Mbeta in the Sutton goal.

Mbeta was given no chance though almost ten minutes later, a few moments before the break. A seemingly still developing situation on the left, for once not primarily involving Dale Binns, saw the ball pushed inside by Connor Maclaren to Dave Taylor. From something approaching 30 yards, he unleashed a real screamer into the top right hand corner of the net to give us a surprizing, if slender, interval lead.

The second half, which successively saw Quincy Rowe, then Andy Crossley, then Jake Baxter take over from Lewis Jackson, Dale Binns and Dave Taylor respectively, swung more in our favour as the minutes ticked by. Gallifent was still not unduly troubled. The closest he came to being beaten was off a headed effort that was palmed away. The Sutton side looked competent in possession but with insufficient ideas on how to unravel the tight Chertsey defence.

In the end, Sutton were lucky not to concede further, this time from more comprehensive Chertsey attacking. A Maclaren, C that is, (brother Kevin did not feature in the game) shot was tipped over. Other efforts ended up with the woodwork being the U's friend when both post from a Baxter strike, and the underside of the bar off John Pomeroy, defended the increasingly vulnerable target as both efforts looked likely to have raised the shout, "goal!"

We ended up the tie the stronger looking outfit. Persistence in defence early on, a well-executed goal out of the blue and taking the game to the opposition in the latter stages deservedly won us a place in the last eight, opponents, as yet, unknown.

Dave Taylor

The scorer of the solitary goal of the game against Sutton United in the Surrey Senior Cup, Dave Taylor is a central midfielder who joined Chertsey Town in the summer of 2018 having played the previous season for Harrow Borough and Cambridge City. He has also played for Northwood and Altona City in Australia. Contributing goals sprinkled

The Mighty Chertsey Town

through the season as well as assists, none was more important than his cup goal that came two and a half months later a long way from home…

Saturday 12th January – CC League   Hanworth Villa 0 Chertsey Town 2
Without hitting the heights, we collected three useful points at Hanworth with a side there that featured seven teenagers. Jake Baxter scored his inevitable (it seems these days) goal on 21 minutes.

After the break, Sam Murphy finished in fine style with 15 to go to take the game to a safer place for us after the home side started to put pressure towards an equaliser.

From the Secretary's Quill

Can I set aside the excitement of the FA Vase just for a moment? It seems to be an annual tradition these days; to see which (usually non-league) clubs will survive to start the following season. There is always great speculation, and some do fall by the wayside, but rarely in numbers that might seem possible at various times of the year.

It might be my imagination, but it feels to me that there are more than usual this time round although only one, and they are at our own level, Blyth Spartans from the Northern League (Step 5), have fallen so far.

There was a big story with Billericay Town (Step 2) before Christmas with their rather controversial owner making waves. Additionally, more recent reports have been heard of recent rumblings from Nuneaton Borough (Step 2) and North Ferriby (Step 3).

Another story is that the owner of Hednesford Town (Step 3) has been trying to step down and sell the club since August, which does not bode well. Nor does the continuing saga at

Ebbsfleet United (Step 1) with players not receiving wages or being covered for injury by insurance premiums.

The situation with Staines Town (Step 3) is not healthy either. It is obvious they will suffer relegation, and if we manage promotion, there is a good chance we could be playing them next season; I hope! My hope in this context is based more on the Swans surviving in their present form more than us rising up a grade.

Underlying all these woes is a sword of Damocles hovering over a collection of clubs higher up the food chain than ourselves. The reason is that minimum dressing room sizes are to be increased from 2019-2020 and all must be in place, or at least robustly set up to be done in the near future, by the end of March. Failure will mean clubs clattering down to Step 5. The potential for an almighty churning of clubs' positions in the coming close season is very real if that threat is carried through.

Of course, many of the dark clouds that loom over the horizon are, and will be this time, mostly blown away but surely there will be wreckage created somewhere. Because the FA insist all clubs finishing bottom of their league will be relegated in any event, so the one for one exchange between Step 4 and Step 5 football will occur. The question is though, how many additional promotion places will be hacked out because of financial/owners giving up/dressing room considerations?

Therefore there could well be a second place promotion on offer in our league as a sort of backstop (if I dare use the expression) arrangement to keep numbers up, but it would be done on a best average performance on a national level. The FA, though, being a law unto themselves, could pull another rabbit out of the bag.

All I can say at this juncture is, thank goodness we are not in a problematic situation – yet! The Dressing room matter could

The Mighty Chertsey Town

> become an issue here, but that would be in a year's time. In the meanwhile, I am going to do my best to enjoy the remainder of our season without experiencing too many traumatic encounters of the 'turd' kind!

Tuesday 15th January – League Cup   Chertsey Town 1 Abbey Rangers 2

We made six changes to our starting line up from three days earlier, plus three regular Under 18 players placed on the bench. This meant that our prime side was not being featured for this League Cup tie. Something similar occurred when Sutton United were in Town, and were overcome, but for this outing, the ploy did not pay off and we were undone by the narrowest of margins.

Both sides though, gave a good account of themselves. An Alex Hendrie free kick was sent over for Bradley Thomas to head home on ten minutes. We replied with Liam Stone in the Abbey goal making a good save and Hendrie forcing the ball off the line after Stone had been beaten.

We exerted pressure after the break, especially and it was the boot of Jake Baxter that put away the equaliser. We looked good for the winner, but it was our next-door neighbours who had the final say with Thomas again the provider on 86 minutes leaving no practical time for us to even the score.

Saturday 19th January – CC League   Chertsey Town 1
**   Camberley Town 0**

In a not very inspiring performance, we just managed to snatch the win against mid table Camberley Town. It looked as if we were going to have to share the spoils until Dale Binns came on from the bench and, in a last gasp move, pin pointed a cross for the boot of Jake Baxter put away the welcome winner.

Jake Baxter

"I joined Chertsey in late September," says Jake. "A good mate of mine Kevin Maclaren was captain here and we had spoken about it pre-season and he was telling me how well the club was run and how much I would enjoy it so I decided to join and I'm glad I did."

Jake started his footballing career with the Fulham Academy, subsequently playing for Cove, Tooting & Mitcham (where he was a prolific scorer) and most recently at Hartley Witney.

During the course of the 2018-2019 season Jake scored five hattricks and six braces, plus numerous single goals. Included in the hattricks was one of his favourite matches of the season, "at home to Knaphill where I scored four goals in the first half and got subbed at half time!"

For Sam Murphy, "The addition of Baxter was huge for the club and me personally. At one stage when I was playing higher up the pitch for a couple of months we were demolishing teams and our link up play was devastating. He proved to be key for us on so many occasions and it was only fitting that he got himself a goal at Wembley."

Saturday 26th January – CC League Raynes Park Vale 2 Chertsey Town 2

Playing on a lunar like surface, and we are not talking about the Sea of Tranquillity here, just a rugged pitch at Raynes Park Vale, we were denied the three points by first conceding a bizarre goal after a minute of play, then another five minutes into stoppage time at the end. Between times, it looked like we had done just enough to claim victory, but a draw was our only reward.

Despite the disappointing score line against opposition languishing at the wrong end of the league table, the afternoon was far from a write off for the standard of football from our lads was high, especially when considering the conditions. It was some inspired goalkeeping from Dan McKelecher that kept his side in the game. Off target Town shooting was also a factor.

Our cause was not helped when, towards the latter end of the first half, midfielder Connor Maclaren was dismissed in curious fashion after an incident with the referee. Thus done, the deficit in numbers was hardly noticed although it must have had a subtle effect in the final analysis. We were a goal adrift by then, one that was conceded in more strange circumstances.

Although yet to see the second minute of the game to pass, we had already made a telling start but with a long Vale clearance, and a cross into our penalty area, Nick Jupp highlighted what a crucial position the goalkeeper holds, with make or break action, and little margin for error between. He looked favourite to gather the cross but the ball slithered from his grasp. Another attempt at the free ball looked to have been successful but again it fell free. This time it was Raynes Park's Ato Okai who got there first and fired the ball home for a shock lead.

We came back hard at the home side with attacks mainly either through the middle or on the left with Dale Binns successfully overcoming both the uneven surface and his marker. He worked a good position in the tenth minute but lingered a mite too long in the crowded penalty area and was blocked. Full back Lewis Jackson had already delivered a fierce shot that flew narrowly wide so it looked a good bet that an equaliser was on its way.

A cross, this time from the right by Mason Welch-Turner found the head of Jake Baxter but the effort was saved close in by McKelecher. Then another Jackson effort, this time a considered curling shot from 25 yards, was tipped over, but only just! We were really on the boil and a succession of corner kicks were won, but in poor consolation for the real prize.

Alice Graysharp with Chris Gay

A strong Michael Kinsella header went narrowly wide and another similar effort from Baxter this time was smartly saved. It looked odds on that Baxter would eventually equal things up when put away with only McKelecher to beat, but slashed the ball wide.

Despite the onslaught, danger still lurked at the other end. A timely tackle by Welch-Turner thwarted a tense moment for Chertsey followers and a reaction save from Jupp from a goal bound shot off the boot of Seanan McKillip stopped Vale's scoring ambitions. But play soon returned to the far end, this time with deserved rewards. A Jackson cross found Binns in front of goal. One touch was all that was needed to set up the well-directed equaliser from ten yards.

The goal was scored on 43 minutes which left just enough time for another rare Raynes Park Vale foray. This time it was Okai again who delivered a sharp shot from a central position but it was met with an even sharper reaction save by Jupp to send the sides into the interval on level terms as far as the score sheet was concerned, but with us well ahead on 'points.'

The second half failed to conjure as many chances but it still looked highly likely that as we were playing all the football, we would eventually break through. The closest effort in the meat of the period came from another strong Kinsella header that went just wide. We were, though, finding it hard to find a chink through the packed Vale bus park!

John Pomroy came on in the 74th minute for Sam Murphy and got the finishing touch four minutes later to edge us ahead for a lead that looked like it was 'job done.' The goal came after a strong run by Dave Taylor who then fired a low shot across the goalmouth. The 'keeper palmed the ball away, but only for Pomroy to clean up.

Our defence, when in position, looked far too strong for the home side. That notion failed five minutes into stoppage time when a free kick on the right, was lobbed in and James Curran was first to connect with his head leaving Jupp with no chance for a most unlikely equalising goal.

Mason Welch-Turner

Full backs rarely hit the headlines but beaver away cutting off crosses, making vital defensive tackles and distributing the ball to the midfield. Mason is one such industrious member of the team, tracking back and pushing forward as part of the defensive line that served Chertsey Town so well throughout the season.

"I joined Chertsey Town half way through pre-season [2018] after playing against them in a pre-season friendly for Hanwell Town," Mason recalls. "I was really impressed with the team they had put together and they wanted to sign me after the game. It felt good to be wanted by a team that was setting out to win the league and try and win the Vase. Another deciding factor was that my dad [Mark Turner] was now part of Chertsey Town and he's watched almost every game I've played in since I was a kid and I knew that wouldn't be possible if I would have stayed at Hanwell Town."

Mason had previously played for Corinthian Casuals, Woking and Hendon. In the FA Vase Final programme, Kevin Maclaren considers Mason "experienced for his age and can be counted on in big games."

Alice Graysharp with Chris Gay

Combined Counties League Premier Division
end of January 2019

	P	W	D	L	F	A	Gd	Pts
Sutton Common Rovers	24	17	3	3	54	28	26	54
Chertsey Town	21	16	4	1	54	21	33	52
Banstead Athletic	26	11	11	4	44	29	15	44
Abbey Rangers	23	14	1	8	41	37	4	43
Guildford City	23	12	4	7	39	33	6	40
Redhill	22	11	5	6	45	38	7	38
Southall	24	10	7	7	39	25	14	37
Spelthorne Sports	25	10	4	11	47	34	13	34
Cobham	25	9	6	10	41	39	2	33
Horley Town	24	9	6	9	36	42	-6	33
Knaphill	25	9	3	13	35	51	-16	30
Balham	24	9	2	13	35	38	-3	29
CB Hounslow United	23	8	4	11	34	37	-3	28
Camberley Town	24	8	4	12	35	41	-6	28
Badshot Lea	23	8	4	11	31	48	-17	28
Colliers Wood United	24	7	4	13	33	45	-12	25
AFC Hayes	25	6	6	13	29	37	-8	24
Raynes Park Vale	22	6	6	10	24	36	-12	24
Hanworth Villa	22	6	5	11	24	33	-9	23
Walton & Hersham	26	4	7	15	33	60	-27	19

Tuesday 5th February – CC League   Chertsey Town 2 Badshot Lea 1
It is said that it is the mark of a good side when they do not play up to their potential but still, through tenacity, come through the test with a victorious result. This was the classic situation when we arguably executed our weakest, and certainly least attractive, performance of the season but somehow snatched all three points against a very competent Badshot Lea side.

The Mighty Chertsey Town

On a drizzle marred evening that did no favours to the playing surface, we struggled to find cohesion with too many searching balls forward frequently finding either the arms of the visitors' goalkeeper or passing harmlessly over the goal line. That thought might be seen as harsh because a whole heap of half chances were created but a reluctance to pull the trigger, off target shots and determined defending created frustration for those with blue in their hearts.

We started well enough. Dale Binns on 12 minutes shot narrowly wide after a loose ball spun to him. Then two minutes later, an over ambitious back pass created panic in a frantic Baggies goalmouth. That was followed up with a Jake Baxter 90-degree flick towards the near post off a low Andy Crossley knock inside, skidding a foot wide.

It looked like success would shortly arrive but, having not threatened at all, Lea took a shock 19th minute lead. A diagonal free kick on the right from Max Herbert was flicked off the forehead of Connor Close into the top nearside corner of the net. The effect seemed to drain us of confidence and our game dropped away, especially in front of goal as promising situations were afforded but soon lost through hesitation. This came at its most glaring just after the half hour when Sam Murphy broke through but the expected shot turned into a pass inside to Baxter but it was not precise enough for a telling strike to be let off with any expectation.

A Lubo Guentchev shot was palmed away as we made a brighter start to the second period but a Badshot Lea break out soon after almost spelt disaster. Full back Sam Flegg, although signed at the start of the season but making a promising debut, recovered to flick the ball away for a corner with a goal looking odds on.

Badshot Lea came back into the game and were better at finding their man. Long range passes out to the left flank were particularly effective but, although with less possession, we looked more likely to score. Despite this scenario, shots were still not quite making their mark. A Guentchev volley was a typical example. It was hit with venom and power from 15 yards, but missed its target, if by a narrow margin.

A push in the back of Baxter by Jordan Clement on goal looked a clear penalty but was not given and it looked like we might fail to score in a match for the first time this season. That prospect was dispelled on 77 minutes when another Guentchev strike failed to hit the net. What it did do though was to thump the ball against the inside of the post and run away to Dale Binns. He had long since switched wings to the right hand side and so was on hand to fire home the equaliser.

Harry Cooksey, having exploited over ambitious play on the halfway line should have done better and put Badshot Lea back in the driving seat but a weak lob stopped that advantage. Instead, the exchange was becoming fraught and on the verge of unmanageable with a series of disruptions and dubious injury calls. It did not upset our side enough to stop the winner.

First the visitors' cross bar was struck, then soon after, one minute into stoppage time of the six allocated, a glancing header by Baxter made sure this time that the net was found, and along with it, our path back to the top of the league table.

By now the weather and the FA Vase were combining to take their toll on Chertsey Town's season. An away fixture to Guildford City of 2nd February had been postponed because of the FA Vase fixture away to Irlam, only for that game in turn to be postposed at a late hour to the following weekend, forcing in turn the postponement of the league fixture of 9th February away to AFC Hayes. Postponed matches were beginning to stack up. However, the second element of Dave Rayner's vision was holding firm and the team travelled to Irlam near Manchester on the first of their long distance away trips in the Vase. All credit, too, to the Chertsey Town supporters who followed them there, especially those on the supporters' coach who had an unexpected pit stop when a coach tyre blew. But they had their reward when they finally made it.

Saturday 9th February – FA Vase 5th Round   Irlam 0 Chertsey Town 2

It was an Irlam defensive error that contributed to us establishing the defining lead that had been threatened over the previous half hour of play. The scene for this encounter was west of Manchester; Irlam to be precise. The prize for winning was a quarter final place in the Buildbase FA Vase.

Niggly injuries affected three of our starters, but the potential problem was successfully concealed and went unnoticed from the prospect of the touchline. Any such disadvantage was more than balanced in the second half when the home side's captain, Charlie Doyle was dismissed for a late flying tackle on full back Mason Welch-Turner as the hour approached.

Irlam set off with the confidence of playing in front of a sizable and vocal home crowd and found the ball more readily in the early stages. Their Liam Morrison fired wide after just three minutes but we won the first corner a few seconds later. The first quarter of an hour belonged to the Lancastrians who displayed menace in attack but failed to open us our defence when it came to the crunch. Their cause was not helped by erratic shooting which became more prevalent as time progressed.

A 20-yard Andy Crossley strike on 13 minutes was comfortably saved by Lee White in goal, but it was a sign that fortunes were on the turn. Irlam's promising start began to fade with breakaway movement out from the midfield being shepherded away from danger spots. Meanwhile, we were having difficulties in mastering raking passes forward. The keen wind was apt to carry the ball beyond targets giving White plenty of collection and kicking practise.

Although their danger man Marcus Perry had a couple of half chances to fire his side ahead, the best opportunity to break the deadlock came at the other end as half time loomed. A Dale Binns run on the right forced the ball to Jake Baxter but his shot on the turn went wide. Sam Murphy surged forward soon after into a prime position to score but his crafted shot failed to fool White. A clip inside to a waiting Binns might, in hindsight, have been a better option.

The interval whistle had yet to be blown as another silk lined chance came our way. This occurred when full back Sam Flegg appeared on the far post, seemingly from nowhere, but headed the ball wide with the home defence out of position leaving a gaping goalmouth.

The second half was, by and large, kept within the domain of our midfield. A goal on 51 minutes helped to maintain an increasing feeling that we had the measure of our opponents. The set up was a gift by an Irlam defender who miscontrolled the ball, letting it slip gently to Lubo Guentchev. He still had plenty to do but did so with aplomb by curling a high ball from the far corner of the penalty area, across the face of goal, and planting it in the upper reaches of the Irlam net. This moment dissipated in a stroke, his recent lean spell to encourage a positive and effective contribution for the remainder of the afternoon

The fortunes of Irlam took a significant dip with the dismissal of Doyle which effectively put paid to serious thoughts of a revival, and they somehow now had to chase the game a man short. The noise from the touch lines, now emanating from us Surrey travellers, almost a hundred in strength, increased when a Crossley, Mason-Turner, Guentchev quickfire combination set up Baxter for a shot that flew narrowly wide. It may not have disturbed the score sheet but was another indicator where the spoils were destined.

Flegg may have disappointingly directed the ball inches wide from the woodwork in a first half attack but was mightily pleased to have arrowed the ball past the crossbar by a similar distance of the very same structure at the far end of the ground, this time in a clearance during a desperate moment when a surprise Irlam strike might have turned the game. It came as their most potent effort of the second period.

The episode illustrated that one goal is never really enough to be completely secure, but insurance cover was fashioned, and came on 89 minutes. Guentchev retrieved a near lost ball on the wing and, with the help of Baxter, forged a pathway to goal. The thrust ended with a push from behind by a very unhappy Morrison.

In result, the confident Baxter spot kick killed off the contest. The following five minutes of stoppage time became an academic exercise in running down the clock. The win maintained our record of scoring in every competitive match this season whilst elevating us into the sixth round of the FA Vase for the third time, leaving just two weeks to prepare for the next stage.

The Vase game against Irlam is Mason Welch-Turner's pick of the season. "Irlam was a big game for us and personally for me it was my first time travelling with the team. We knew of Irlam's quality and we knew if we were to beat them we would be serious contenders for the Vase. It was a big game for me as Dave and the staff paid so much attention to Irlam's right winger I knew I had to play at my best to stand a chance."

Alice Graysharp with Chris Gay

From The Secretary's Quill

I was going to write about sentimentality in football this week but more current events, as far as we are concerned, have pushed that topic to one side. So in changing subjects, I have no idea what I am about to spout about except the general subject of the FA Vase and my recollections, so this is an exercise in spontaneity for us both!

The inauguration of competition coincided with me joining the club's committee in 1974. I was the reserve team mother hen that season so did not witness our first ever tie. My first came in the January. It was the fourth round so we were not doing too badly. I can remember the game vividly with the assistance of one word... Mud!

It rained and rained that weekend but, as usual, ours was the only game on as the pitch was just about playable, even though it was decidedly not so, after 46 boots had simultaneously churched it up, come 4.45pm. (22 players and one referee = 46). Our spectating facilities were not as sophisticated as today either.

The then clubhouse was set back further from the pitch than now and before it lay a gravel patio which, in wet weather, stuck to your shoes. There was a narrow concrete path along the touch line from the stand to the corner flag but pretty well everywhere else was welly boot terrain.

Our opponents that day were Marlow, a high flying Athenian League club then, well above our level. We were doing well that season (came runners up in the league) so still fancied our chances but a weather related, stuck in the mud moment, aided our visitors to a 1 – 0 win in the rain over us.

I could not wait to get home that day. It was not so much of the result, but more because of the conditions. You can imagine what the clubhouse floor looked like, let alone the state the dressing rooms. You could not escape from 'brown' anywhere.

The Mighty Chertsey Town

> My plight was exasperated a few minutes before half time. The tea bar is where the dressing rooms sit now. Also the area in front of the stand was out of bounds for spectators, being where the players entered the field of play. I was carrying a tray full of already poured mugs of tea to the dressing room via the front entrance when, on stepping round the corner, met the full force of a misdirected football.
>
> I was thus subjected to more 'brown,' but this time tea! This little interlude brightened some Curfews supporters (we were the goal down at the time), but not this one. It was not my favourite moment of my life at Alwyns Lane.
>
> I have had plenty more FA Vase downers since then. I was nearly violent with one of our players in 2006 with his incendiary flippant could-not-care-less comment after we had chucked away, in what I considered at that moment in a slaphappy manner, a two goal lead, to lose the match and along with it, desperately needed prize money.
>
> I have enjoyed the highs too, not always due to winning through to the later rounds, but that helps. The mere prospect of playing a Vase match is always uplifting. I have seen over 80 such games and the percentage of memorable events surrounding these ties is far higher than in any other competition encountered. It is my favourite.

Tuesday 12th February – Surrey Senior Cup　　**Walton Casuals 3**
　　　　　　　　　　　　　　　　　　　　　　　　　　　　　Chertsey Town 1

Southern League Premier Division side Walton Casuals paid us the compliment of fielding their full side in this Surrey Senior Cup tie. We made wholesale changes due to this game being sandwiched between two key matches, but still gave good account of ourselves. There was, in the end, a two-goal gap, but the game was much closer and a draw with its resultant penalty shoot-out could quite easily have occurred.

Alice Graysharp with Chris Gay

Walton Casuals had three 'goals' knocked out by the offside flag but still took a two-goal lead with successful strikes, each on the break, firstly from James Ewington on 25 minutes, then Max Hustwick two minutes later.

The danger that the home side would then run away with the fixture could have been a possibility, but our game improved minute on minute to put us in command leading up to half time. Good football was executed and it looked like we were at last getting used to playing on an artificial pitch, a surface that has proved in the recent past to not suit our normal game.

A searching Lubo Guentchev run through the middle almost worked but he was shut down by a posse of defenders, but we had better success on 44 minutes with more attractive play that eventually saw Andy Crossley lay the ball across into a space just outside the Walton penalty area. There, Dave Taylor made good first time contact and seemed to steer the ball into the top corner of the net from 20 yards.

We started the second half with a bang. A delivered corner kick was met on the volley by Michael Kinsella in front of the Stags goal but the ball was heaved too high. That was our best effort of the second half in front of goal but there was plenty going on deeper on the park.

One more goal was conceded, on 80 minutes in frankly disappointing circumstances. A couple of opportunities were on offer to put boot laces through the ball to clear in a very precarious position but an attempt to play away with style was attempted, and undone leaving Taureen Roberts with an easy tap in and bye bye to our Surrey Senior Cup journey.

Earlier, Walton had squandered a couple of golden chances but blasted the ball over the bar when in prime position, but any further Walton goals would have cruelly distorted the score

The Mighty Chertsey Town

line for us. The two-goal gap probably gave sense to the balance of the game.

Saturday 16th February – CC League   **Chertsey Town 2**
Sutton Common Rovers 2

There was plenty of spectator interest in the top of the table clash when Sutton Common Rovers came to restrict our title ambitions. The fans, 238 of them, were not let down. A competitive afternoon, with a match played in good heart with no upsets, and controlled well by the referee, presented entertainment well beyond Step Five football. The match ended in a draw which suited us the best given the league table situation.

We were the first to put on pressure. Placing Jake Baxter wide in place of the injured Dale Binns put Sam Murphy and Lubo Guentchev inside at the front. Captain Kevin Maclaren again played an effective pivotal playmaker role. The early pressure paid off after just ten minutes. The ball was lofted into the Sutton goal face where a pinball game was played out. Goalkeeper Ollie Ellaway managed to palm three attempts from inside the six-yard box away but not Dave Taylor's decisive header.

Only two minutes of supremacy was enjoyed before Sutton Common struck back. A left sided corner kick was headed on by an attacker. The ball was not cleared and it then fell to Daryl Cooper-Smith on the left who fired in a rocket shot to bring the scores back into balance. The game continued to be open with us working shorter passes whilst Rovers favoured raking dangerous looking 40 yard passes into our territory, particularly to the right flank.

Why Baxter failed to put us ahead again midway through the half was a mystery. He made tremendous progress in possession through the middle, even passing Ellaway, but the final ten-yard stab lacked velocity which allowed Guy Baskerville to race back and clear off the line with our crowd howling for a goal! Another goal line clearance, this time more comfortable for the defence, was needed to keep Sam Flegg's header out from the resultant corner kick.

Andy Crossley sustained a harsh yellow card before the break which became significant after the interval when, on 65 minutes, a really justified late tackle yellow was shown to him, to reduce us to ten men. But with action still flowing in the first half, we showed more striking ambitions. A Baxter-Guentchev move set up the latter but he fired over, as did Murphy after receiving a pass cut back by the busy Baxter.

We continued probing right from the restart following the turnaround. But it was Sutton who initially came closest when a glancing header by Marlon Pinder was clawed away by Nick Jupp. The referee's whistle blew with purpose when Ollie Twum fell in our box but a potential spot kick gave way to a yellow card for diving. Another heart stopping moment came on the hour when a point-blank range header by Matt Farrell was miraculously saved by an instinctive Jupp for what must rate as the save of the season in anyone's book.

Now a man short, our task looked stiffer but the onus was on Sutton to secure the three catch up points. They tried, they really tried, and were running with the tide with us hanging on. Their task took a turn for the worse though on 81 minutes when we struck back. A Rovers' clearance was blocked and a corner kick ensued. From it, the ball hit three heads, the third being the decisive one as Taylor struck again in similar fashion to his first, to edge us ahead once more.

Also in similar fashion, Sutton replied within two minutes. A lofted cross from the right saw a completely unmarked Twum head past Jupp. Four minutes of stoppage time was played out with high energy, still with neither side trying to run down the clock. The residual eleven minutes might have brought a winner, more likely in the visitors' favour, but unsung defensive heroes again played a vital role with bricks and mortar determination to maintain their resolute wall. The draw was a justified result; it left us the happier side, still in command of our own destiny.

Nick Jupp regarded Sutton Common Rovers at home as "massive as it was them who were our only title contenders and we went down to ten men and managed to get a result which meant that we kept daylight between them in the league, a very important point."

Getting his first red card in the home game against Sutton Common Rovers was for Andy Crossley the lowest point of his season "which meant that I was banned for the quarter final." Hopefully the team would see their way through the coming tie, and with league games to also absorb the ban Andy would be back in the squad in time for the semi-final. But first there was West Auckland in the way…

West Auckland

A restless night of dozing and waking, paranoid I'd miss two alarms set for 4.30am and admitting defeat at 4.20am, an hour later I crept out of the house in the darkest part of the night, driving through fog on the A3 and wondering whether I'd dreamt the whole sign-up-for-the-6.15am-supporters'-coach-to-West-Auckland-for-Chertsey-Town-FC-in-the-FA-Vase-quarter-final thing.

It wasn't the first time I'd done crazy things for football – a day trip to Zagreb and a coach and ferry overnighter to a Europa League Final with a Premiership Club in the past – but, for Chertsey Town?!! The furthest I'd supported Chertsey winning away was at Walton & Hersham (ahh, that wicked Jason Tucker free kick and me the only Chertsey Town supporter in the Stompond Lane stand) or losing away at Sutton United, back in the old days of the

ICIS Premier League. I'd missed out on Irlam away the previous cup round and was determined to make this one but it felt surreal. So as I neared the top of London Street I was much relieved to see two people walking in the Abbeyfields direction, one of whom was wearing a Chertsey Town shirt.

Hanging around at the end of Colonels Lane, not even a bird's tweet to presage the morning, I spotted a small group starting to gather at the far bus stop. The attendance list was checked by Sam Harris (to whom a huge vote of thanks is due for shepherding the Chertsey flock to the long distance away games), then 6.15am passed with no coach in sight and Dave Rayner in Darlington rudely awakened by Sam's call enquiring as to its whereabouts. A 30-seater eventually trundled up for the fifteen hardy souls shivering in the pre-dawn gloom. Setting off around 6.45am and settling down for a good sleep on the first leg, the journey was punctuated by two brief stops with West Auckland's football ground reached at around 1pm.

I headed off in the direction of an intriguing tea room I'd recce'd via the internet – Antiques on the Green doubling as Molly's Tea Room. After admiring the contents of a central glass antiques display cabinet it was time to consume an enormous doorstep of a sandwich. "HAM & PEASEPUDDING A Northern delicacy!" proclaimed the menu. "Beautiful slices of roasted ham accompanied with tasty, locally made Peasepudding". Being an ignorant southerner I thought peasepudding only echoed in nursery rhymes, but here was my chance to try something indigenous. "You can learn something new every day" is one of my mottos and I certainly did – for a start, peasepudding isn't green, it's yellow, and it makes a great spread to put in sandwiches. Accompanied by a generous side salad and crisps, washed down with lashings of tea, all for under a fiver. Then out onto the sun drenched green to admire the

The Mighty Chertsey Town

local architecture and to photograph the statue celebrating West Auckland's claim to fame.

"Sir Thomas Lipton Trophy – The Original World Cup" proclaimed the plaque above which a footballer, leg outstretched, arms flung out for balance, was in the act of booting a ball above a pickaxe-grasping figure sprawled sideways on the plinth. "Final played in Turin on April 12th 1909 West Auckland 2-0 FC Winterhour (Switzerland)" the etching continued. Making a mental note to undertake further internet investigations, I retraced my steps to the WMR Stadium ("WMR" standing for "Wanted Metal", I later learned, so that was clear then) and was enlightened by the programme that West Auckland were winners of the first World Cup in both 1909 and 1911. Unfortunately it was not a money spinner and the cost of two trips to Italy for the competition led to the club folding in 1912 and the 'World Cup' being sold off to meet its debts.

The glorious sunshine was deceptive and in the shade of the stand a chill wind drew hat, gloves and an extra layer out of my rucksack, then Chertsey Town were running out, resplendent in their blue and white home kit, and the serious business of the day began.

**Saturday 23rd February – FA Vase Q Final   West Auckland Town 0
                                                                           Chertsey Town 2**

Our quarter final opponents in the Buildbase FA Vase were the bookies' competition favourites prior to kick off but have subsequently been replaced by the ourselves after the win and passage into new territory; the semi-final of a national based competition. It was a tie that produced two distinct characters with the half time providing the dividing line. Both, though, set up, then kept, us in the ascendency.

We out played our hosts in the attacking game during the first 45 minutes, to construct a two goal lead, almost without a meaningful reaction from the County Durham side. However, they took their pick axes from the locker at half time and dug into a strong response to press against our attributes which, as seen in previous displays, mined a rich seam of endeavour to deny West's continued interest in the competition.

The unseasonably warm conditions of sun and a benign breeze was the only bright feature exuding from the Wanted Stadium as the home support were eerily muted at the start and continued, increasingly more understandably, in that vein throughout the exchange. In contrast was the sound from us sixty or so travellers, mostly congregated behind the opposition goal. We had plenty to shout about!

The lively Chertsey Town start was underlined after ten minutes with a goal; the first decisive moment of the game. It was sublime action as Kevin Maclaren, 35 yards out on the right, swung in a high diagonal ball that Dale Binns developed with an amazing touch that left his marker out of bounds. The moment was concluded with a low 12-yard unstoppable strike.

It took until the 15th minute before any evidence of an attack by West Auckland was evident, whereas we took every opportunity to pump the ball forward. This momentum continued and generated more success on 27 minutes. It was another well-crafted goal that commenced with a Sam Murphy free kick deep on the left flank.

The ball was met by the head of Quincy Rowe who directed back inside to Dave Taylor. The penalty area proved to be too congested to get a shot away but Rowe was found to the right where he found a gap to fire in low just inside the post from ten yards. A multi-combo effort shortly after set up prolific marksman Jake Baxter. His shot was first blocked by Shane Bland in goal but the rebound, with the shooter under pressure clipped the wrong side of the upright.

The Mighty Chertsey Town

West Auckland Town showed far more ambition in the second half, to push us back into our own territory for extended periods. However, their attack, despite creating corner kicks that pushed a total into double figures, lacked sufficient invention to break the resolute defending. Adam Burnicle, off the bench, came closest with two good efforts, the first smothered by Nick Jupp at close range; the second skidded narrowly wide.

Jupp was plenty busy but mainly in plucking out the ball from the dangerously looking crosses department, but that is not to say the back line failed to do their bit. It was a real team effort in the deeper recesses of the well-maintained park. The main discomfort of the second half was that so often, clearances fell straight into the feet of an amber shirt. This did not spell disaster, but merely prolonged a forlorn hope by the home side that they might just manage a breakthrough by attrition, but it was more in hope than expectation.

The clock further leaked away chances of a comeback for the northerners and so our victory came to pass. The result produced a happy journey home, just as well given the distance, but there are plenty of miles yet to consume if we are required to find a way to North West London.

The scorer of Chertsey's second goal at West Auckland, central defender Quincy Rowe pounced and his goalbound strike was as rare as it was stunning. Whereas a one-goal difference might have kept the game open, the second goal gave Chertsey a cushion with which to absorb the onslaught of the second half. Quincy rates the West Auckland game as one of his top matches of the season, not only because he scored but also because it "was our best defensive display all season, it felt as if we could have been playing all day and they weren't going to score."

West Auckland away is high on many of the players' matches of the season list. "They were the favourites and were a club steeped in history," says Kevin Maclaren. "Physically their players were big and strong and from the highlights we had seen they looked to be a very effective team. We won the game in the first half and defended excellently. All of our players put in a good performance and I believe that's the game where it became reality, that we were possibly the best team in the competition and could go all the way."

For Dale Binns, too, "travelling to face the tournament favourites was massive. At the time I had been suffering with a hernia injury which had limited my involvements in games and training. It was touch and go if I was fit enough to start. I did and scored what I believe was one of my most important goals of the season. The boys played a tremendous game and to leave with a clean sheet showed how far we had come but also gave us the belief that we can go all the way."

Defender Lewis Jackson picks West Auckland as "my most memorable moment where I dealt with their 'most dangerous player' and it helped towards our run to the final at Wembley and was our best performance defensively."

Dave Anderson recalls, "It was the first time I felt we could win the Vase and said so quietly to the staff. We learnt something about ourselves in that match, going 2-0 up in the first half and defending well in the second. Sometimes it's easier to play than watch. On the pitch you're wrapped up in what you're doing. That second half at West Auckland felt like four hours, not forty-five minutes!"

The Mighty Chertsey Town

From the Secretary's Quill

I cannot continue my Quill notes without entering FA Vase territory. I was cornered by the BBC last week for a short interview about my ambitions for the club. I mentioned I had three but in fact I really have four. The fourth is for a stable club that can hold its own at Step 3 or 4 without having to look over its shoulder. Any higher, then the whole is quite a different ball game.

That ambition, although very important, is a bit boring to contemplate at the moment, don't you think? I have dozens of, 'we have somehow survived another season,' tee shirts clogging up my wardrobe so it will great to have another design for a change.

The survival notion sits in its own category but I suppose third place in the other 'fluffy' category is us reaching the first round proper of the FA Cup and travelling to a good Football League club (giving a good account of ourselves of course). Brentford used to be the target, but it could end up with the likes of Reading, the way they are going at the moment!

Second on the podium will be to win whatever league we are playing in. I can remember Chertsey Town lifting such trophies back in my prime but that was 55 years ago. It is about time we had our name scratched on a championship trophy again. We have been elevated for various reasons, eight times during my tenure on the committee, but always as the bridesmaid, as it were, never the bride. Touch wood and whistle; that ambition has a good chance of being realised at last.

Top of the list though must be seeing Chertsey Town run out at Wembley. The FA Cup is out, as is the FA Trophy (for now!). That just leaves the FA Vase, but I am not picky so that will do just fine. Seeing MY team trot out onto the hallowed turf, as they say, would be a dream come true. To end that day with royal blue ribbons on the trophy and being held aloft by a familiar face would be a bonus.

Alice Graysharp with Chris Gay

> It is not just the 90 or so minutes of football that would bring so much pleasure but all the accompanying trimmings. The après football hullabaloo that goes with such an occasion will bring just as much pleasure; a feeling of being part of something special in a relatively exalted position with which to harbour memories for years to come.
>
> I know, as secretary, it will not be all rainbows and candy floss. There is a hell of a lot of work involved with preparations, involving the team itself, administration, corporate and financial opportunities, publicity, public relations, staffing and other esoteric pressures yet to be realised. This aspect has already started and we are still 'only' at the semi-final stage.
>
> A discipline that began some three rounds back was to not to get ahead of myself so I am dampening internal speculation. One thing I have done that I thought was stupid in the past. Well, I still do think it is daft; that is superstition, but I have taken to wearing the same blue and white pinstriped shirt, but only for Vase matches. I am only hoping I will be wearing it with purpose in HA9 in a couple of months' time. Dreams can come true, even if it is just a once in a lifetime experience. I am not greedy, so just the once will do me okay.

Chris Gay is not alone. Superstitions abound in football, players and fans alike. Dave Rayner "wouldn't shave until we got knocked out of the FA Cup and as it turned out I barely had time to grow a stubble! Also with 15 minutes to go in a game I like to go behind the opposition's goal where the players can hear me urging them on, I think we've scored a lot of our goals in the last fifteen minutes. And from the last sixteen of the FA Vase onwards I took to wearing a suit, and as I would usually turn up to matches in jeans I got some ribbing from the players!"

The Mighty Chertsey Town

Some players' superstitions are ingrained early. Lewis Gallifent has "quite a lot of superstitions, I always put my left glove on first, I always have to use the same water bottle from the warm up throughout the game, my water has to be in the right side of the goal and I have to be on the six yard line when we kick off."

Fellow 'keeper Nick Jupp explains about his purple kit. "In the first half of the season the only games we lost I was in green so I made a point of wearing purple as much as I can. I also have some small superstitions where I have my bottle on my left post, and rub grass from my goal into my gloves each half."

Quincy Rowe too has "loads of football superstitions. If we win I do everything the same before the following game including having the same breakfast, eating at the same place, and even down to the order I put my socks on. And I only wash my boots if we win. And that's why I usually turn up at the last minute as I like to time everything the same! Lubo has a superstition that he always has to come out last. We've tried all kind of tricks including someone hiding behind the door but he's wise to them. It must have worked because he's been a brilliant player."

While Jake Baxter doesn't feel he has many superstitions he admits to "putting my left shin pad on before my right and when we are warming up I make sure at the end when we are takings shots at the goal that my last one is a good strike that hits the back of the net."

Mason Welch-Turner too doesn't regard himself as having superstitions, "but I made sure I prepared for each and every game the same no matter who we were playing or where we were playing." And for Andy Crossley, "If I have had a good game I try to do things exactly the same the next match."

"I washed the captain's armband after each match once we started winning," says John Pomroy, "and continued this throughout the season."

Perhaps more of a habit than a superstition, for Michael Peacock "Whichever club I play I always stick to the same spot in the changing room where I first sit and I don't move."

And if Danny Bennell doesn't "turn up to football with an energy drink, water and a bar of snickers or mars, I don't feel I'm fully equipped to get through." I know the feeling – and I'm just a spectator!

After the high of the Vase quarter-final win, the following Tuesday, 26th February, saw a return to the bread and butter of the league at home to Redhill, a 2-1 win with Dave Taylor and Lewis Driver scoring for Chertsey. This trend continued the following Saturday.

Saturday 2nd March – CC League   Chertsey Town 4 Balham 1

In an almost routine dismissal of Combined Counties League visitors Balham, we collected another three points to come within one of leaders Sutton Common. In scoring two early goals, we almost put the game to bed before the nearby St Peter's parish church had struck the quarter hour.

So it was a happy boss Dave Anderson, come 4.45pm. Well, not exactly! There was a visible desire by the whole team not to find their way into the referee's book and perhaps a subsequent suspension over the FA Vase Semi-Final 'season.' That quest was successful. However, two dark clouds settled themselves over Alwyns Lane after the game, one more menacing than the other.

Andy Crossley, in midfield, turned his ankle over and was carried off the park. More profound though was the injury to Michael Kinsella who was also lifted off the pitch. The injury was later confirmed as a fracture of the ankle. It could see his season is over; a devastating blow on a personal basis to him, and hardly the best of news for the team which will be under severe manpower pressures for the remainder of the season.

As for the game itself; this was a more sparkling affair than seen of late in our league performances. Was it a co-incidence in that attacking midfielder Lubo Guentchev also got his mojo back? He snatched two goals with a confidence not seen for a few weeks. His well-executed goal after just six minutes set us on our way. A diagonal cross from Lewis Driver was tamed by Guentchev who, from the edge of the penalty area, lobbed the ball over Balham goalkeeper Haydn Read.

It looked all too easy two minutes later when a right flank precision cross from Guentchev was headed home in front of the sticks by Crossley. Our dawn raids certainly caught out the half-asleep Londoners who seemingly were still contemplating their navels. Thus, all was going well until midway through the half when Kinsella came out of a tackle in great physical pain, later to turn to a mental one after the prognosis on his ankle. Danny Bennell replaced him on the park.

Apart from a moment almost on the half hour when Nick Jupp was forced to palm aside a useful shot at distance from Tom Read, that took a potentially fatal bounce just in front of the diving goalkeeper, we had complete control of the contest. However, only two prominent goal scoring efforts were mounted before the break when Driver unleashed a powerful strike from the 18-yard line that took a deflection but was saved, then in the final moments, another from the same forward, this time a header which at was again saved under pressure.

Balham regrouped after the turnaround but without much penetration as our defence, as usual, again did a job on the opposition. Dale Binns replaced Driver, who is still building up his match fitness after his four-month layoff. It made a significant difference. Eight minutes after the swap, we increased our already secure lead. Guentchev recorded his brace from ten yards after some right-wing magic from Binns, who was far too quick for his marker.

The three goal lead almost became four a couple of minutes later with a Bennell off target header. Guentchev then looked odds on to secure a hattrick with a rasping shot through a crowded Balham penalty area but ironically, it was Jake Baxter that got in the way to divert the strike. We increasingly dominated in the latter stages with an off balance Guentchev shot and John Pomroy's effort on the swivel off a Kevin Maclaren feed, both coming close.

An arid period over the past weeks by his own prolific standards ended for Baxter in the 85th minute. Binns again proved to be the catalyst with speed and guile on the right for the league's top marksman to slide in number four for us. It was Balham, however, who had the last say on the rebound. A counter attack through the middle got Balham's big front unit, as they say, on the ball. With defenders bouncing off him as he honed in on Jupp, James Adebayo put away a consolation goal in the last action that still left us in a deservedly comfortable position.

Tuesday 5th March – CC League   **CB Hounslow United 0**
Chertsey Town 4

Ensrettet, Einbahn, Le sens unique, Senso unico. Whichever language you might care to use, traffic during our league fixture at CB Hounslow United was only being directed one way; into our hosts' half of their superbly presented pitch. This was a comfortable win that hoisted us back on top of the table with an even more comfortable margin in the table over the sides left in their wake.

Apart from two yellow cards being issued, the evening at Green Lane was almost text book. Our forward movement was relentless and the only criticism that might be levied was that there were too many instances of trying to walk the ball into the net. But that often happens when sides are overwhelmingly on top. Although there was plenty of energy in the performance, it was well that this was only physical and not mental for there is still a long road ahead, even if it is routed along the sunnier side of the Surrey Hills.

Any murky outlook emanated only from the news from the previous outing of Michael Kinsella and Andy Crossley's injuries. The main change to the line up from the previous weekend was Fred Hill starting at full back for Mason Welch-Turner, and Danny Bennell, in for Dave Taylor. Player protection, as well as collecting league points, was the order of the day.

Despite the balance of possession and promise of goals, only one was scored before the interval. It came on 13 minutes from one of the myriad of corner kicks forced. Dale Binns delivered from the right flank. Jake Baxter headed on and Bennell completed the operation close in with another header. There was so much sharp passing from us, so it was strange that few direct and accurate attempts on goal were forthcoming. The closest at this stage was a Baxter volley, one of three seen during the 90 minutes, that fizzed wide.

The second period brought a better return for our dominance. The CB Hounslow side are at the wrong end of the table but showed glimpses of good football but they were unable to sustain momentum. A sequence of three or four passes had the potential to cause problems but our defending quickly snuffed out the danger. Nick Jupp was only called up to make one telling save, late in the game after the result was beyond question.

In the meanwhile, Baxter secured a hattrick of goals, his first for two months; an arid period in his book. His first success came three minutes after the restart. A throw in on the left, some 25 yards out started a sequence that involved Lubo

Alice Graysharp with Chris Gay

Guentchev, Dale Binns, then Kevin Maclaren, before the quick-fire movement being signed off a few feet from goal. The two goal lead hardly looked a vulnerable situation but patience had to be exercised before the gap could be increased.

A far post volley from Lewis Driver off a fierce Guentchev delivery whistled past the post on the hour. The same supplier, a quarter of hour later sent Baxter away to give Kavanagh Keadell in goal with no chance. The 'keeper did well to parry a strong Baxter shot that took a slight deflection, but he was unable to stop the fourth, secured in the 79th minute. The goal came from the penalty spot with the Chertsey number nine as executioner. The kick was awarded for a sneaky hand ball that was not sneaky enough. It took place in the extremities of the Hounslow area, and not in a particularly dangerous situation; a bit of defensive silliness.

It did not make a material difference to the result but helped to give a permanent illustration of the difference between the two sides. It also assisted in recording a full year's cycle in the club's life. It was a year, almost to the day, when manager Dave Anderson took over and took a cobbled up side to be beaten 5-1 at the same ground. That followed a walk out of almost all the then squad which was patched up within four days, later leading us to greater things.

Northwich Victoria away in the Semi-final of the FA Vase coming up on 16th March. The furthest stage in the FA Vase ever reached by Chertsey Town, a not-to-be-missed-once-in-a-lifetime event. So my sister in Dublin booked her flights, rented an Airbnb in Gogmore Lane for two nights and I booked us two places on the supporters' coach for the away leg. But Storm Gareth had other ideas. Heavy rain had led to the postponement of the league match away to Banstead on 9th March, then Storm Gareth hit the UK over the night of 12th to 13th March and away to Guildford

City on 13th March was also postponed. Surely, though, a couple of days' grace after that would be enough. But as I drove off on a calm, bright late Friday afternoon to join my sister in Chertsey for the weekend my mobile pinged – Chris Gay was spreading the word of the match's postponement. Storm Gareth was refusing to lie down in the North.

Storm Gareth's cloud had a silver lining for me and my sister as we'd not been together in Chertsey for forty years and the next morning after a late breakfast at Joe's café and a raid on Chertsey Museum we morphed into tourists in our home town. Following a small Chertsey guide book we explored the site of the Abbey and its sparse remains, taking photographs standing in the solitary surviving doorway, following the line of the Abbey boundary ditch extant in Willow Walk, and comparing London Street buildings with those remembered from decades before including the baker's opposite the Town Hall (demolished in the late 1970s for the new road) where our mother bought miniature Hovis loaves to keep little fingers and mouths occupied in the pushchair on our way home from the shops. And rounding the day off with another nostalgic trip to the cinema at Staines, though in a different, new, location and Fisherman's Friends instead of Diamonds Are Forever.

While we were able to make the most of the disappointing postponement, Chertsey Town's players endured another weekend of frustrating inaction. For Quincy Rowe the semi-final postponement "was a downer as I was all geared up for it and there was no midweek match and it worked out that we didn't play for two and a half weeks and I couldn't mentally switch off."

WINTER 2018-2019

Jake Baxter (foreground)

Jake Baxter with Golden Boot award

The Mighty Chertsey Town

Mason Welch-Turner

Mason Welch-Turner shielding the ball

Jake Baxter (number 9) goalbound at Irlam

Quincy Rowe defending at Irlam while Andy Crossley (left), Kevin Maclaren and Nick Jupp (right) look on

The Mighty Chertsey Town

Chertsey Town supporters at West Auckland

Team huddle at West Auckland

Chertsey Town's first goal at West Auckland from the boot of Dale Binns

Safe in the arms of Nick Jupp at West Auckland

The Mighty Chertsey Town

From the boot of Quincy Rowe at West Auckland

Quincy Rowe celebrating his goal with
Dave Taylor at West Auckland

SPRING 2019

**Sunday 24th March – FA Vase Semi-Final 1st Leg   Northwich Victoria 1
Chertsey Town 1**

Our quick return to the North West saw us come away undefeated in the first leg of the FA Vase Semi-Final. The cagey match created limited opportunities for either sides and felt more like a prelude to the main event, to take place a week later. We had the edge as far as chances, or rather half chances, were concerned, but our hosts will have taken comfort from a strong finish.

A more than brisk breeze, that predominately raced down the length of the pitch, did neither side any favours. We started off with it at our backs which resulted in the ball flying off well in advance of chasing feet with either goal kicks or, more acceptably, throw-ins at the corner recesses of the ample pitch being the dominant feature of the early exchanges.

The first half corner kick tally was won by ourselves, but it was scant reward for the main objective. However, it was from one such situation that a bizarre lead was almost created. The ball was curled towards the near post by Lubo Guentchev but in a desperate attempt to clear the knee high ball, a Victoria defender sliced the ball in the wrong direction and was mightily relieved to see the upright save the day for potential blushes.

In forcing a way into the headwind, the home side hardly bothered our back line which either mopped up with efficiency, showed power in the air or was adept at stealing possession before any dangerous situations could be mounted. It was important that we built some sort of rampart to defend when the time to turnaround came. Question marks began to appear as the break loomed, but then, the deadlock was broken.

It came on 41 minutes with Dale Binns breaking through on the right from where he centred the ball. Jake Baxter made an awkward connection that merely projected the missile further on, but no nearer to goal. All was not lost for Guentchev then collected and returned the ball into a congested goalmouth where Dave Taylor got the vital touch to stab home.

It was then, after the turnaround, Northwich Victoria's turn to overcook forward passes and there seemed little danger of Nick Jupp in his newly presented orange goalkeeper's kit being sullied with the likes of full-length saves. Protection at the back was tight, but the same could be said of the home side. This balance continued to produce little in the way of goal mouth incidents, which favoured us the better of the two.

A momentum was building out of the Surrey camp midway through the period. A 22 yard free kick, central to the goal, from Guentchev clipped the wall to safety. Binns had a couple of strikes that comfortably cleared the cross bar, but despite a great deal of off the ball movement, we still failed to cleave open a clear-cut chance with only a couple of weak shots to show which hardly warmed the hands of Daniel Taberner in their goal.

It was at this point the game suddenly swung in the opposite direction. A raking clearance to the right on the break saw the ball launched over the back to Harvey Whyte. He cut in and from six yards, at only a slight angle, fired a vicious shot past Jupp who was beaten for pace. This equalising goal came on 71 minutes and put heart into the home side's resolve. They started picking up loose balls in the manner we had done earlier but despite a final 20 minutes of expectation by the home fans, their side never seriously challenged the status quo, but nor did we in our now less frequent approaches to the Trickies' deeper territory.

After the final whistle the Chertsey Town players made a bee-line for their supporters behind the Northwich Victoria goal, shaking hands with the fans and high fiving. Despite the disappointment of conceding an equaliser to the hosts, the Chertsey Town players were upbeat. "We'll win it at home," they said. Their self-belief was infectious and their team spirit evident.

This team spirit was enhanced by the camaraderie of the long distance away trips with this being their third such consecutive FA Vase outing. "The trips away were quality," says Andy Crossley. "The club, Dave Rayner and Barney [Mark Turner] arranged them brilliantly and everything was set up for us like professionals." Lewis Driver agrees. "It was all done very professionally and made us feel we were playing at a lot higher level than we were."

For Michael Peacock, "The best thing about our long away trips has got to be the journeys back, a few drinks and plenty of sing along, the team has a real togetherness and we all had a real laugh travelling home. We were also very privileged to travel to the games on the Virgin Trains which is the most comfortable away travelling I've had. Another highlight would be actually playing teams you would never normally get to play and playing teams with a bit of unknown about them and this has brought the best out of me this season. I roomed with Dave Taylor a lad I've known for 13 years or so, I used to play football with his older brother and used to stay round their house all the time and playing football in the garden and kicking him about a bit, but now he has pay back in training and I've played against him a few times and he actually split my eye open, but he's a good mate and a good roomy."

Sam Flegg "loved spending time with the lads – it's the best group of players I've ever played with. The team spirit was great and everyone got on really well."

Jake Baxter's favourite part of the away trips was "Hawkes' quizzes, they are brilliant." Quincy Rowe concurs. "The best thing about the overnight away trips was the quizzes run by

Steve Hawkins, they did wonders for team morale which was really good anyway and the quizzes made it even better. While there were no cliques in the squad some players tended to gravitate towards some more than others. The quizzes mixed everyone up and you got to know players even better. It sometimes got a bit heated, though, with a couple of players squaring up to each other, which was hilarious!"

Mason Welch-Turner's favourite part of the overnight trips "was being able to share the time with my team mates that you usually wouldn't. You could see how everyone prepares for games and you can get to know everyone that little bit better."

For young Lewis Gallifent the whole experience was about "being around everyone and having a good laugh." At the other end of the footballing spectrum, Dale Binns confirms the very special experience. "Barney and Dave Rayner really looked after the boys, with the travel and accommodation. Then with Hawks' evening quiz, Gaffer's stories and speeches and then to having a few drinks with the boys on the way back, those were some great away days. I can honestly say it was up there with teams I played for in the Conference."

Nick Jupp also highlights the team spirit and the evening quizzes. "Just being away with the team is a privilege as everyone has become genuine friends. The highlight of the away games is always Hawkes' quiz that he does for the team and my team always win. Quincy Rowe is my roomy and he is an absolute gem of a bloke, we always have laugh together. On our first away trip he fell asleep on his bed all night fully dressed, shoes included!"

Kevin Maclaren praises both the organisers and the supporters. "The treatment we received from the club on our away trips in the FA Vase this season will live long in my memory. They left no stone unturned in ensuring we were treated like professionals and I feel it really benefited our performances.

From the pre match meals, to Steve Hawkins' legendary quizzes, to morning walks, it was an experience like no other. Full credit must go to Mark Turner for arranging it all and Dave Rayner for putting his hand in his pocket. We had such great turnouts from the Chertsey supporters too. That didn't go unnoticed by the players and it gave us that extra few percent which makes the difference in the big games."

There were a few drawbacks to the long-distance trips. As a PE teacher and Head of Year Quincy Rowe was concerned about the Friday travelling as he would not normally be allowed the time off, "but I was lucky, I was let off." One player owned to missing his family; another roomed with a player who snored. Mason Welch-Turner found that "the worst part of the overnight trips is just the waiting for the games. It seemed like forever from the Friday to the game at 3pm on the Saturday which build a bit of tension for the game but it also helps you focus on the game more." For Jake Baxter, though, "The worst thing about the trips is when they're over, stepping off the train after singing the whole way home."

The work that went into organising the away trips was all undertaken by unpaid officials of the Club, primarily Mark Turner. Despite the pressures, though, Mark "loved every minute of the away trips. At Darlington [West Auckland away] we went to an outside nightclub. You went through the door and stepped out and it was like at some Spanish resort. There we were outdoors at midnight in February drinking beer. And it was five drinks for a tenner!"

Dave Rayner praises "the great team spirit and self-discipline of the players. Steve Hawkins would run a quiz night then at 10.30 he'd tell them to go off to bed and they did without exception. One of Dave Anderson's rules was no women and the players respected that. Of course the rest of us lived it up, one night some didn't get to bed till three or four in the morning, but there were no complaints from the players. On the way back after the match it was different, each player had to get up the front and sing and we bought cases of beer. On all three trips we were the underdogs so the return journeys were especially enjoyable."

In the matchday programme for the home leg of the semi-final, Chris Gay referenced some of the hidden work that goes on in the background.

From The Secretary's Quill

Setting up games such as the one we have today commands much more organising than the sum of its components. That might seem both a convoluted and obvious statement, but in having to address all the side issues and dealing with various agencies, it has reminded me how complicated staging football matches can become.

It is probably easier if done regularly with an established routine, but as we are all at the club, have had to plough new furrows. It has not always been a smooth passage of the past month, but we have worked well with each other and challenges have been overcome quite quickly; team work!

This has also highlighted how clubs, who will be doing their best to do each other no favours on the park will, outside the 90 minutes, also strive closely together to make the day work as best as possible. Our game with Irlam was a prime example. Home supporters will recall the original match had to be postponed for seven days. This caused so much hassle as hotel bookings, train travel and local coach hire arrangements had to be undone at the last minute, then rebooked; a nightmare.

Thankfully, Mark Turner took the brunt of all that, but for my part it took a lot of close liaising with the Irlam secretary in the lead up to the postponement. Decisions had to be taken early and with focus as the then deadline was AM the Friday before.

Because we have a special programme edition today, which required much of copy to be submitted to the printer before last Saturday, these notes had to be written almost two weeks ago, at a time of some trepidation experienced because of persistent and storms in the days leading to the first leg of this tie. Plans may have profoundly altered by the time today's game should be played, not reflected in these notes. Fingers are crossed as I write these notes; not easy to do at the same time!

In this matter, the two clubs have also got together with a number of pre-match understandings. Dave, the Vics' secretary, and myself have had a good relationship. Good communication and co-operation is essential. Recent events in our own league have reminded me that this does not always occur. It is very frustrating to bang your head against a brick wall when dealing with others who are on a different wavelength.

My thrust is that the football world is a great fraternity. It can get over sentimental or over excitable with matters that should really command a lower priority in our lives, but common sense eventually reigns in most cases. Staging football is not easy, but the co-operation and friendship exchanged is all worthwhile.

I have a primary three peaks ambition for the club I have supported for almost sixty years. Playing a Football League club in the first round of the FA Cup, a league championship and a Wembley appearance. Two could be done this season. In waffling on about background tasks, I have not forgotten our players' and team management contributions in setting up this exceptional this season. Their efforts are also to be applauded at today's peak of achievement, so far experienced as a club official.

The Mighty Chertsey Town

A huge crowd of 1,847 gathered, over 600 more than for the away leg, to see whether Chertsey Town could make history. Again, as already the team had taken them further in the FA Vase than ever before. With me in that crowd was my sister, flown in on a day trip from Dublin, meeting up earlier for lunch at Joe's Café with the high street ringing to strains of "Wemberlee, Wemberlee" emanating from the Prince Regent next door, a palpable sense of cup fever hanging in the air.

Saturday 30th March – FA Vase Semi-Final 2nd Leg   Chertsey Town 0
Northwich Victoria 0

Our side had scored in every competitive outing this season during open play So it was with some irony that we succeeded this time, but without finding the net in open play to, nonetheless, record victory in the biggest game in the club's considerable history. Opposition was provided in North West Counties League side, Northwich Victoria. As a club, they had already tasted the delights of playing in Wembley finals. It was done three times in the past, vying for the FA Trophy, but were a more modest outfit on this occasion.

Two hours of open football failed to produce even one goal by either team so that the tie had to be resolved in the cruellest way. A penalty shoot-out in a second leg of the FA Vase semi-final is not the best way of deciding who wins the big Wembley Stadium appearance prize, but that is how things are decided these days. It was ourselves that edged the contest and so progress to realise the dream of seeing our team walk out onto the hallowed turf.

The game itself was conducted in a sporting manner, but was very competitive. It created few goalmouth incidents, and when it did, both goalkeepers were masters in their realm. Both stopped odds on winning strikes towards the end of the game. Failure to have done so would almost certainly have spelt expulsion within minutes.

Alice Graysharp with Chris Gay

In fact, Nick Jupp went one notch further in saving one of the penalty shots in the game's appendix which, with the involvement of five strikers of course, effectively sealed the tie in our favour. It is right to state, 'tie, and not 'game' because the Alwyns Lane show was part two of the greater saga, following the one a piece, first leg draw at Northwich.

There was still an element of caginess left over from the opening leg but both sides had a number of promising semi created opportunities. However, defences mounted at each end remained the dominant forces and it was indeed only half chance scraps that were on offer. It would be debatable where the balance lay in that field.

We had our best spell towards the end of the 90 minutes when it would be fair to state that it was the away side that were the happier of the two, to hear the interim 'final' whistle. Almost inevitably, extra time provided for the best chances as legs began to tire.

Somehow, both goalkeepers kept those late efforts out with miracle saves, Dan Taberner from Lewis Driver and Nick Jupp from Robert Doran, to push the game into the final spot kick climax.

We won the prize for taking the first kick. The sequence went; Jake Baxter 1-0, Dominic Craig 1-1, Lubo Guentchev 2-1, Ryan Winder saved by Jupp still 2-1, Dave Taylor, 3-1, Brian Matthews 3-2, Andy Crossley, 4-2, Robert Doran 4-3, Sam Murphy 5-3 and victory! Murphy was later nominated the Chertsey Town Man of the Match with Nick Jupp as a close runner up.

"***Spot-on Curfews seize their Wembley Dream***" screamed the sports headline in the *Surrey Advertiser*. "***Wembley Joy for Curfews***" proclaimed *The Non-League Paper*.

For Sam Flegg, "The second leg of the Vase Semi at home to Northwich Victoria was pretty special. I didn't think we played all that well, certainly nowhere near as well as we could – but to win on penalties in front of a huge home crowd was pretty special, especially with the reward being a trip to Wembley."

Lewis Driver rates the semi-final of the Vase second leg "as a game I'll never forget. Wembley was amazing but winning a game that takes you there has to be up there!"

Lubomir Guentchev thinks "both the quarters and semis in the Vase were special as it takes character and team spirit to make it through both rounds. Having to travel up north against two very good teams and to get the better of them overall, is something thing special. It says a lot about the boys and everyone involved with the club."

And for the scorer of the penalty that put Chertsey Town through to the Final, "scoring the penalty to send us to Wembley was probably my personal highlight [of the season]. I felt so confident when it went to penalties as I have scored in play off final shootouts and have a pretty decent record from the spot. I said to Dave I want the fifth penalty as I knew it would get to that stage. When it came round everything in my head went to full focus and I completed blocked out the crowd. I decided as I walked to the ball where I would put it and that was it. I gave the 'keeper the eyes and as soon as I hit it I knew we was on our way to Wembley. A great moment for me and the club in front of a record crowd."

Sam Murphy's match winning penalty was the signal for a pitch invasion with jubilant fans running, galloping, leaping, air punching and embracing the players and each other. Yelling, chanting, shouting, whooping, they exhaled the tension of the shoot out and inhaled the heady cocktail of victory and sheer relief that Chertsey Town's players had done it. Lewis Gallifent nominates the semi-final second leg as one of his matches of the season "because after that game there was just a great buzz and atmosphere and with all the fans running on the pitch, it was great!" Chertsey Town Football Club was going to Wemberlee.

But first there was the small matter of wrapping up the league title…

**Tuesday 2nd April – CC League   Colliers Wood United 3
                                                                     Chertsey Town 3**

With a feeling that anything was possible after such a momentous weekend after winning through to the FA Vase Final, there could have been a danger of taking a mere league game as an aside, to let the prize of points slip easily away. The packed schedule that wedges in three games a week to the end of the season as the norm meant that Dave Anderson needs to nurture his squad though some testing times.

He began with only fielding two starting players that did the same three days earlier. Kevin Maclaren and Sam Flegg was the duo of names in the frame. So it was quite a different line up that began the game, but with a very familiar mind set in how to face up to our opponents. We did our best to play on the floor football, helped by a flat pitch but one that was soundly rinsed later in the game by sharp and intense storm showers.

All went well at the start but in trying always to play out from the back was our undoing. Robbery occurred on 31 minutes when possession was lost just outside the penalty area whilst trying to play a too sophisticated brand of football instead of putting lace through leather with gusto. Mario Embarlo has been the thorn in our side for many a season and became their enemy number one again but taking charge and planting the ball home from 15 yards.

Although we more than matched their hosts in open play, matters became worse after conceding a free kick ten yards outside

The Mighty Chertsey Town

of their penalty area. Although the ball did not penetrate from the kick, effective clearance was not achieved and play quickly returned to a central position just inside the box. From there, a shot from Will Entebe almost trundled pass a phalanx of legs and into the corner of the Chertsey net, leaving Lewis Gallifent frozen out.

It was thus a two goal advantage to South West London come 41 minutes, but that gap was reduced to one by the time the half time whistle was blown. A free kick was given away on the right flank where Andy Crossley delivered. The ball flew high into Wood's goalmouth. It was not effectively cleared but fell to James McCuskey, one of the players drafted in the combat squad fatigue. He made his mark in stoppage time by pumping the ball into the net from a good 15 yards.

Our fortunes rose further in a second half of few openings. An equaliser came just seven minutes into the period. This time it was Glen Yala acting as the catalyst. His deep delivery from the right arrived low in the Colliers Wood goalmouth where an under pressure defender tried to steer the ball out for a corner but only manged to slide it into his own net.

It looked like a point was going to be snatched from the encounter but, on 80 minutes, the home side fired back into the lead. In becoming stoppage time aficionados though, we scored a vital goal beyond the 90-minute mark to pull the game back once again. It was Crossley again who turned provider from the wing. His high ball was met by Jake Baxter, who had come off the bench to replace John Pomroy, then headed into the net to edge us further towards the top of the table.

Away to Colliers Wood was Sam Flegg's lowest point of the season, "on a cold and wet Tuesday night on a terrible pitch. I was held up at work so only just made the game and started terribly. I gave the ball away for their first goal to go one up. We ended up drawing the game but it was a poor night for me personally."

Being held up at work can be an added complication for non-league players over full time professional footballers. Having to rush to games from work for Sam Flegg, who works in central London as a Finance Consultant, means he doesn't have time to prepare for midweek games as well as he can for Saturday matches, though the reward is that "football is a great release for me and it's a totally different environment to what I experience during the day."

Dale Binns also found midweek games a rush, doing the after school and nursery run following a working day before dashing off to football as soon as his wife arrived home.

In contrast, John Pomroy is a postman, "therefore Saturday was often a rush but midweek was easy as I finish early."

Andy Crossley has also found Saturdays can be affected by work. "I work in a bank so it's quite difficult with Saturdays but I've not had to miss any which is great – I just get a few late fines!!"

Michael Peacock sometimes has to miss matches for his work. "My day job is an engineer for Openreach/BT so providing lines and fixing them mainly for broadband, so people are usually delighted to see me as most people these days can't live without the internet. My manager has been a great help this year, I have to work one Saturday a month which is a bit of a pain, but he managed to move hours about to make me available for the FA Vase games and big league games."

Sam Murphy has found his work can clash with his commitment to football training. "I work in Mayfair in the Ralph Lauren head office and the long hours and regular work travel meant that I could no longer commit to playing at the level I was with Hendon. It seemed like the perfect timing when Kev asked me to come down to Chertsey and help him out. Dave was a brilliant manager and I'm gutted we never got to work together before. Not only was he brilliant on match days, but he was really understanding when I couldn't make training due to work commitments. He knew I would keep myself fit in my own time and we built that trust."

Jake Baxter is "an electrician and it has been really easy as my boss is a football fan so understands it all and he has been really fair and understanding if I've ever had to leave a bit early."

Also an electrician is Mason Welch-Turner who works in central London. "Football is a big commitment no matter what level you play at so you find yourself having to leave work early to make training and games. Luckily for me I work for my dad so I'm able to leave early without getting into much trouble."

Kevin Maclaren finds his job as a London taxi driver, which means he is self-employed, "perfect for football because I can pick and choose my hours. It's a job I've done since my 21st birthday and I was the youngest person to ever complete 'The Knowledge' which is the test we have to pass to get our licence. I was still only 19 when I passed this and had to wait over a year until I was old enough to drive a cab. It can be a lonely and unhealthy job at times! Sitting on my bum all day hasn't done my football career any good. Only means you put on weight easier and get more injuries as your muscles are less active.

"I've picked up a few famous people. Hugh Grant, Rowan Atkinson, Paul Weller, James Arthur and a few others. I don't really talk to my passengers much. I speak when I'm spoken to but would never try and spark up a conversation.

I'm of the view that everyone wants to be left alone and would rather scroll through social media than talk to me about the weather!"

Next London taxi I grab I'll be checking out the driver, just in case…

For Lewis Driver, though, being self-employed can have its drawbacks. "I'm a carpenter by trade but run my own small building company called LDF Solutions Ltd. It's difficult because working for yourself people presume you can work when you want but the real case is more like you never stop working. I normally work most Saturday mornings, I've done it at every level I've ever played. Even before big cup games."

Thursday 4th April – CC League   Banstead Athletic 1 Chertsey Town 2

We hardly scaled the heights at Merland Rise but still managed a narrow league win over hosts Banstead Athletic, not made any easier by a glaring second half miss following, a little after the hour, the dismissal of Kevin Maclaren for an alleged loose elbow. A win, and not primarily the performance, was the order of the day so Dave Anderson will be satisfied with the final score line, if not the fact his captain would miss four future league matches.

The team formation returned to a more familiar set up with the usual gang kicking off, although Dale Binns, later to come onto replace Lewis Driver, initially sat on the bench. Sam Flegg was the other absentee with Lewis Jackson taking the number two shirt with the two players seemingly to be taking alternate turns in the full back position.

The game began positively enough with us taking the initiative, initiating plenty of play just outside the Banstead penalty area. Although no direct strike at goal was achieved at that time, there was plenty of scope for success, which turned out to be

The Mighty Chertsey Town

true on the quarter of an hour. A through ball from Jackson in midfield was ignored by Jake Baxter who was in an offside position. Instead, Lubo Guentchev ran past the back line, to his right of the goal to take charge.

After taking the ball to the bye line, he squared it back into the path of Lewis Driver who had no difficulty in thumping it past Jack Minchin in the Banstead goal, in a flowing movement that could have been choreographed by ***Strictly***'s Bruno Tonioli. Well perhaps that is an exaggeration, but it was a slick move that could not be countered.

It looked like we were well on their way to a comfortable evening with our opponents confined to speculative counter attacks, but any thoughts of complacency were shattered just nine minutes later when a corner kick from the Banstead left was turned in by Joe Cheeseman, just a few yards on the near post.

Apart from a Dave Taylor headed effort that went wide being the closest to a goal, both sides tried but did not seriously threaten until stoppage time arrived when, almost on cue, a Chertsey Town goal was struck. This had an even better crafted finish with four players knocking the ball around the Banstead goal environs. The home side's defence looked solid but were eventually pulled open to allow Guentchev to take full advantage by piling the ball home from ten yards.

The slender lead was hardly put under pressure after the break with Nick Jupp in goal being busy at times but never in trouble. Meanwhile, we could hardly be said to be setting the world alight at the other end either. The best moments of the game were confined to the first half.

A Taylor volley right in front of goal that saw the ball skied at a 45-degree angle over the bar did not seem a critical miss at the time but minutes later a goal at that moment would have been very handy. The reason was that, in an almost deft moment in midfield with no pressure being applied by either side, the referee interpreted a jutting elbow to be deliberate so Maclaren was obliged to leave the field.

In consequence, Guentchev was replaced by a more defensively solid Glen Yala. That, with width in attack being sacrificed by Binns tucking inside instead of his wide station, a more claustrophobic final stage to the contest was engineered. This favoured us the most as we were able to maintain their lead without too much trauma and with it three more points.

From where I was watching, Kevin Maclaren's challenge seemed innocuous enough but the ref had other ideas. It was to the credit of the team's never say die attitude that they ground out a win despite losing their captain. Banstead away was Kevin Maclaren's lowest point of the season. "I've had a chequered history with my discipline on the pitch throughout my career. I've really tried to curb it and was sent off at Banstead for something that in my opinion was ridiculously soft. I was very angry and frustrated with myself, the referee, the opposition's players and let that get the better of me. I let everyone down. Luckily we had more or less won the league at that point so the resulting suspension didn't make too much of a difference however it could have been very different had Sutton Common Rovers put us under more pressure in the latter stages of the season."

Saturday 6th April – CC League   Badshot Lea 0 Chertsey Town 3

We returned to the top of the league table with an emphatic victory at well placed Badshot Lea. The result seemed expected after observing just a few minutes of play, even though the first goal took 35 minutes to arrive and was all that separated each team on paper at half time. Badshot Lea provided a game performance but we were invariably a degree or two stronger.

The Mighty Chertsey Town

The recent introduction of James McCluskey was continued, giving a strong emphasis on our attacking strength. Fred Hill was drafted in at full back to make a useful contribution while Quincy Rowe and Mason Welch-Turner were unavailable. Dave Anderson, once more, applied his options within the recently expanded squad, to great effect.

Controlled and promising football, mostly but not exclusively by ourselves, graced the opening minutes, but without any real threat being created. The first potent break came on 21 minutes when Sam Murphy on the right, advanced the ball to Lewis Driver. He in turn, quickly found Jake Baxter but the marksman's effort to find the net was too weak to trouble Jorden Clement in the home goal.

Nick Jupp at the other end was forced to save at full length to prove that traffic was not all one way, but we came back again. Kevin Maclaren fired one over the Baggies cross bar but with better accuracy, and how, soon after. Murphy again delivered from the right hand corner. The ball looked to have shot over awkwardly as it went closer to the edge of the penalty area than the goalmouth, but the direction turned into a good choice.

Maclaren was lurking unmarked outside the box and from there he unleashed a half volley from the outside of his foot that sent the ball away from Clements into the top corner, and with it a deserved lead. Baxter looked as if he was about to increase that lead a little later but the home goalkeeper denied the chance with a goal line save with his foot. Badshot Lea were made to work hard, and succeeded, to keep the score down as half time approached.

Lubo Guentchev might also have found the net once play resumed but his header went wide. Then a chipped effort by Driver off a James McCluskey feed from the flank was saved. An almost spectacular Lea defensive error that saw possession at left back turn, via a looping misdirected pass, into the domain of Guentchev in the centre of the park. He was able to set up a strike at goal, but one that was again turned aside for a corner kick.

Badshot Lea failed to properly clear the ball from that kick and another cross from the other side gave Sam Flegg an unmolested chance to head home, which he did with aplomb. Clements for once was unable to stop the seemingly inevitable. This two goal lead was established on 66 minutes, but that did not last for long; just three minutes in fact. Our third was then despatched to put the game to bed.

Another quick-fire sequence of passing, this time on the far reaches of the left flank, resulted in full back Fred Hill sending over a precise cross for Baxter to head firmly home, directing the ball into the top corner of the net, well clear of flaying arms. It signalled a slight sway towards the home side gaining an edge. Our defence, resolute all day long, continued to keep heart failure fodder for spectators comfortably under cover though.

The closest to a reply from the host side came from a strong 20 yard strike from Danilo Cadete that forced Jupp into a full length save, but one that looked well within his repertoire. Strong defending and midfield play was again outstanding to help our created the platform for success.

Sam Flegg

The scorer of Chertsey Town's third goal away to Badshot Lea, Sam Flegg signed from Tooting and Mitcham, although most of his career previously was with Hendon and before that with Thatcham Town. A full back, he was described by Kevin Maclaren in the FA Vase Final programme as "one of the best defenders you'll see at this level and is a triathlete, so is as fit as a fiddle." Sam's goal against Badshot Lea proved not to be his only goal of the season…

The Mighty Chertsey Town

Tuesday 9th April – CC League   Cobham 0 Chertsey Town 2

Two awarded first half penalty kicks put Jake Baxter in the spotlight. One was put away on the half hour but the second, set up soon after, was saved by the 'keeper. The youthful home side put up strong and enthusiastic resistance but rarely looked to pull the game back in their favour. This was confirmed with Baxter finding the back of the net again, this time in open play, on 62 minutes not only to add to his total and become the league's top scorer, but also to ensure another three points went back to Alwyns Lane.

Alwyns Lane

Chertsey Town FC takes the name of its ground from the lane in which it is situated. The lane is known to have existed by the early fourteenth century when it appeared as Halewyneslane, and variously in later centuries as Hale Lane, Colt Lane and Meeting House Lane. An Ordnance Survey map of 1860 calls it Chapel Lane, with a "Congregational Chapel" and "Willats Almshouses". A chapel existed in the lane from at least 1704 and was replaced in 1725. It was Presbyterian-Congregational chapel and lasted until 1877; its burial ground is still there, a curiosity tucked behind the residential street. Almshouses were erected by a Guildford Street grocer, Thomas Willate, in 1837 of which two survive.

Originally a cul de sac, in the 1880s Alwyns Lane was connected to the 1850s built Grove Road. It remains an eclectic mix of old and new with a modern office block across from eighteenth century elegance at its opening, a mini 1950s development opposite the almshouses halfway down and small street-fronting terraced houses nudging the ground, a microcosm of the town of Chertsey itself. At the far end of Chertsey Town's ground nestles a 1980s development that opened up former Gogmore Farm land providing a playground where the roar of the crowd can be heard on matchdays.

Football came to Alwyns Lane in 1929, prior to which the club played at Willow Walk, Free Prae Road, Staines Lane and Chilsey Green. The ground was donated by Sir Edward Stern to the "premier club in the parish". Beyond the west side of the ground lies the cricket club whose ground was similarly donated. The main stand was constructed in the mid 1950s, the original clubhouse added in 1960 and the first covered enclosure was built in 1963.

Saturday 13th April – CC League   Chertsey Town 5 Southall 1

Our visitors did not deserve to have such a penalising score line recorded against their efforts. Conversely, we did not deserve overall to reap such an emphatic league win. But the final score will be etched in stone for ever more, justified or not. We certainly deserved the win though as we took one more step towards our seeming unstoppable march towards the championship.

Southall, for much of the game, gave as good as they got and it was only in the final twenty minutes that they were swept aside by conceding four goals. Although we always had our noses in front, a sustained effort after the interval put questions marks against the destination of the points. Direct play in particular from raking runs by Darreon Mark, started to cause problems for the defence.

Although Southall scored during this vibrant post interval period, poor finishing at other key moments let us off the hook. Play was then pulled round in our favour to set up the runaway victory. The sun was shining that afternoon, but its rays fell especially on Lewis Driver who hit a hattrick, and John Pomroy with a brace of goals, despite only being on the park for the final dozen minutes.

The Mighty Chertsey Town

There was no Quincy Rowe, no Kevin Maclaren, now on suspension, no Michael Peacock and no Glenn Yala in the day's squad. One of Dave Anderson's management tasks is to keep his extended squad of players all happy as he side picks it way through the dense thicket of catch up league matches, playing mix and match to maintain freshness. This he has managed to good effect.

Freshness was evident from the start, even if little in the way of goalmouth action came of it; indeed it was Nick Jupp who was the first of the two goalkeepers to be called into action with a full length save on 20 minutes after a mini flurry of action from Southall. That moment seemed to kick start our scoring ambitions for we established a lead only two minutes later. It was a quick-fire series of passes between Jake Baxter and Dale Binns that was finished off by Lewis Driver.

Two unfortunate Southall injuries, one involving a dislocated shoulder, broke up the game for a while as extended treatment was administered but the game returned to its former pace. This happened first with Driver firing wide on the turn, then Southall sub Damel Dioum worked a great position only to see his close-range shot ricochet off the shoulder of Jupp.

The same defender was forced to act in a sweeper's role as Mark honed in soon after the break with Southall again pressing. Sanard Fernandes was permitted a run across the outside of the penalty area before turning to fire a low shot into the corner of the net for what seemed at the time an unsurprising 56th minute equalising goal. Southall still looked good for another goal but our defence regained full control and blue forward movement became more prominent.

Driver then bagged his second goal with a volley close in, almost falling into the ball, off a Sam Murphy left wing cross to regain a lead that became ever solid. The Driver hattrick could hardly have said to have been constructed; it was a gift, although well taken. Louis Daley, the Middlesex centre back, took a wild swing at the ball in an attempt to clear, despite no real pressure. It fell to Driver a few yards away and he pushed forward into the box, then curled the ball round Rourke Pickford with a quarter of an hour still on the clock.

By then Fred Hill had replaced Binns. Driver was swapped with Pomroy soon after. Another glaring miss, this time by Southall's Ricardo Faux-James might have given a tighter finish to an already completed contest but instead, we inflicted further punishment at the other end. It came from the right with Andy Crossly centring the ball, to be collected by Dave Taylor. This movement completely shredded the Southall defence which allowed Pomroy to finish off with a 12 inch tap in.

Baxter usually finishes off goal scoring movement but again was the provider in this exchange. With two minutes still remaining, he set up Pomroy who swept the ball home from ten yards in the style so often seen from him over the years. It was a vintage finish to a contemporary moment that placed us just three points away from the championship.

Lewis Driver

The hattrick hero against Southall signed at the start of the season. In his late twenties, the striker brought the experience of his years at Burnham, where he won promotion with them to the Southern League Premier Division in 2013, at Harrow Borough and, most recently, at Staines Town. "Dave asked me to join after playing for him at Harrow, I'd actually retired due to a serious knee injury and a couple of professional opinions. However, he convinced me to come and see Gary Anderson for a third opinion, and before I knew it was on an operating table and spent two months on crutches!" He was disappointed to miss the big games while out injured, especially "not being fit enough to start in the first leg of the semi."

The Mighty Chertsey Town

Lewis worked hard to get back to form in time for the closing matches of the season. "At home to Southall scoring a hattrick after being out for six months was a very sweet moment." Coming on as sub in extra time of the FA Vase semi-final second leg, he featured in the starting line up for the FA Vase Final. In the FA Vase Final programme Kevin Maclaren says, "The impact he's had is special. He's brilliant in the air, hangs like a salmon and is very vocal in the dressing room."

Tuesday 16th April – CC League　　　AFC Hayes 1 Chertsey Town 3
AFC Hayes provided the scene for celebrations to confirm our place as Combined Counties League champions for season 2018-19. We have ridden through quite some peaks and troughs since their last championship, in 1962. The wait for such success has been a long time a coming and for a short while on the night, might well have been turned into an even longer wait.

Early goals can settle a team, and push it on to victory. So with one under the belt after just nine minutes, we might well have set the seal in a game against relegation haunted strugglers. The game in the second half, lost its way after AFC Hayes snatched an equaliser. It took a while but then we eventually found the gears again and completed proceedings on a high with two late goals.

The congratulatory banner was then allowed to be unfurled as Champagne sprayed some of the 147 witnesses as soon as the final whistle was blown, to create a happy finale to the evening for Chertsey Town player and supporters alike. The game still left a gruelling half dozen more matches in order to complete their league programme but no rivals can catch us now.

It is not easy to know what the optimum Chertsey Town line up is these days these days. The compact series of games has forced a rotation system into the squad. It is perhaps easier to

Alice Graysharp with Chris Gay

check who is not amongst the starters. Included in that list on the night were Dale Binns, Kevin Maclaren, Sam Murphy and Mason Welch-Turner. The latter was there, waiting on the bench, as were John Pomroy, Andy Crossley and Sam Flegg.

Hayes started with a warning with Nick Jupp in goal forced to dive full length off a headed effort but moments later the up field action was more decisive when Quincy Rowe found Lubo Guentchev. He, with a bit of space, let fly with a speculative 30-yard strike which hit the inside post and crossed the line behind the astonished home goalkeeper.

Spurred on, we pressed forward and within five minutes, Jake Baxter skewed wide from a good position and then a cross from the right missed by goodness knows how many players before Fred Hill on the far post made a connection, but only managed to connect the ball with the post. The game then lost some form with only a flashing 15-yard strike from Lewis Driver as a late highlight before the interval.

After a bright start to the second half that saw a Baxter volley go over the bar, our game inexplicably fell below par with passes going astray and the home side being allowed to collect too many loose balls. Their extra possession eventually helped set up the equaliser which came on 55 minutes. The Hayes marksman Sekana McCalmon found a way through a crowded Chertsey defence and slotted home from close range.

Fallow football continued, raising the home side's hopes of an unexpected point, whilst slowing down the game at every opportunity. Completion of the contest came following a series of Chertsey substitutions. Firstly with Hill exchanged for Crossley on 66 minutes, Glen Yala by John Pomroy in the 75th, and, two minutes later, Flegg came on for Driver. All those replaced had good outings but the exchanges introduced a new dynamic into the performance.

The Mighty Chertsey Town

Goals soon followed with a cheeky Crossley back heel on 79 minutes from next to the penalty spot after collecting the ball from a blocked Lewis Jackson goal attempt, meaning we were back on to quickly confirm the championship once more. This was further underlined eight minutes later by Jackson himself in sneaking up on the right and heading home unmolested by the far post off a perfect left flank cross from the side of the penalty area by Guentchev after left wing movement from Baxter.

That just about did it! Our lads can be proud of their achievement in picking off the title still with six games remaining, and with a bonus to their season of the Wembley Vase appearance to top off a remarkable turnaround in the club's fortunes, especially compared to the struggles over the past seven seasons.

For players and fans alike this was an evening to savour. Jake Baxter reflects,

"Dave [Anderson] always said to us anyone can win a cup competition but the best teams win the league so when we won the league it was a great feeling. I think we all felt halfway through the season that it was ours to lose so was nice to do it in style as we made sure with quite a few games left in hand, which then gave us a lot of time to focus on the FA Vase final."

Thursday 18th April – CC League **Chertsey Town 4**
CB Hounslow United 2

Another Combined Counties League game, sandwiched by two others spread over just five days, resulted in an inevitable change of personnel on the park. The line-up may have been radically altered from the one that saw the championship win two days previous, but the end product was much the same. An encouraging start, followed by a sterile period, followed by the overwhelming of the opposition. In this case, it was Alwyns

Alice Graysharp with Chris Gay

Lane visitors CB Hounslow United who had chances to upset but eventually succumbed.

Patient Nick Jupp understudy, Lewis Gallifent defended between the sticks and had an unblemished performance that earned him the Chertsey Man of the Match Award. Arlie Talboys, from the Under 18s for his first appearance since November after a loan period away, came in at right back and fitted in well. Sam Murphy, rested last Tuesday returned for a very busy and effective time in the midfield. His inclusion as a starter was one of seven made by team boss Dave Anderson. It created some disjointed football for a while in the first half, but the plan came good after the interval.

Our busy start was usurped by a goal from the opposition. Kai Hamilton showed speed and agility all evening and received an early reward in anticipation with his effort on 13 minutes when he tore through the left side, worked through to goal, and almost tapped the ball home. It pepped up Hounslow's efforts; a combination of swiftly shutting us down when in possession, and a lack of belief by the home side by pumping ineffective speculative 30-yard passes forward.

Gallifent was called in to make a full length save, but then the frailty of the away side, who are engaged in a relegation battle, showed through. Completely out of the blue, three defenders, some forty yards from goal messed up between them. The moment was sized upon by Murphy who quickly gained possession of the ball then delivered it to Andy Crossley. He forged towards goal and planted the ball past goalkeeper Kavanagh Kavendish, to equal up the score on 34 minutes.

The first half ended on a positive note with another goal to ward off a worry that a shock defeat might be a possibility. It was a typical Curfew moment of magic with the ball worked on the left and swiftly crossed. It forced Kavendish to almost play volleyball with the 'keeper twice palming the ball from Dale

The Mighty Chertsey Town

Binns and John Pomroy but with the latter killing off the rally for a 39th minute lead.

We were much better connected after the break and returned to sharp passing movement. The result was from more incisive football. Lubo Guentchev came on for Binns as the speed of play markedly increased, but it was not all us. Gallifent made a brave block at the feet of a Hounslow forward. He also got a fingertip to a free kick that found the woodwork instead of the back of his net.

But the visitors did break through on 77 minutes with Luke Dunn sweeping the ball home from 15 yards, after taking advantage of some sparse defending. Soon after, Lewis Jackson came on to replace Crossley. Two minutes later, the 82nd, he was to be found on the score sheet. A Guentchev corner kick from the left planted the ball right in front of the sticks. A furtive scramble took place where Jackson got the final touch by stabbing home from just a few yards.

It is fast becoming a tradition that we score when the 90-minute mark is hovering about. First though, came another great save by Gallifent with the ball looking destined to put the game back on level terms. The confirming Chertsey goal was another well-constructed effort with Fred Hill finding the left side. A Murphy dummy created space for a Hill to continue and cross. The ball was met by Pomroy who put the ball away after another defence splitting move.

These latter goals gave a greater shine to the performance than seemed likely some 60 minutes earlier. However, this was another reconstructed line up which could have prompted excuses but none were needed. It seemingly matters not who from the greater squad is out there.

The win against CB Hounslow ranks for John Pomroy up there with the championship winning match at Hayes and

the FA Vase Final because "CB Hounslow at home was when I scored the last goal for Chertsey. This was the 347th goal and the last time I scored for Chertsey."

I was privileged to be the match sponsor for the home match against CB Hounslow. April 2019 was for me a celebration of 50 years since my first attendance at Alwyns Lane. I have Lord Baden-Powell to thank for this. By the 1968-1969 season I was allowed to stay up late to watch Match of the Day and I wanted to watch live football. But my mother was adamant. "Football matches are not suitable places for young ladies, let alone young girls!" My Guide Handbook provided the inspiration. One of the Self-Training Schemes required, "Go to a type of entertainment that is new to you – circus, ballet, concert, play etc." I'd been to all those and my maternal grandfather attended Chertsey Town matches, so the argument was simple – the Guide Handbook said I should go to a football match and my grandfather could take me.

My mother eventually relented (she told me years later that she only agreed because she thought it would get football out of my system!) and so on a sunny 5th April 1969 my grandfather took me to Alwyns Lane. I don't remember who we played or the final score, only that I'm sure Chertsey won. I loved every minute of it. I remember standing along the side in front of the stand thinking this was the best thing I'd ever done. Afterwards my grandfather told my mother, "She's got quite a voice on her!"

I must have enthused enough for my sister to want to join us, and she also recalls our father taking us on occasion. By our mid-teens we were going on our own. Like me, she remembers that in summer, early autumn and spring you could sit in the stand and watch the cricket being played in the distance at the same time – no high fir trees then – with footballs bouncing onto the cricket pitch.

The Mighty Chertsey Town

Ironically, when I sponsored the Match Ball on 14th October 2000 in memory of my father, my mother came as my guest and said afterwards that she had very much enjoyed the day (perhaps being treated like royalty in the Boardroom contributed!).

Saturday 20th April – CC League   Abbey Rangers 1 Chertsey Town 0
For the first time in this season's Combined Counties League challenge, we failed to find the net. It resulted in defeat by the only goal of the game at next door Abbey Rangers. Nothing can be taken away from the host side's win, but the only goal, well taken in its execution by Bobby Main, was a gift of sorts when the ball got away from the feet of the Chertsey defence, with no danger lurking and well away from goal. The striker, once in possession, ran the required 35 yards and lofted the ball into the roof of the net.

So it was a local derby with two teams at the rarefied end of the league table. Seven yellow cards were issued. Therefore, it must have been a blood and guts affair with the sides going hammer and tongs at each other and the referee working hard to keep the lid on. Well, actually, no. The game far from a stroll, despite playing under full sun during the hottest Easter period experienced in decades, but it was not full on which made it difficult to understand why so much yellow was flourished, and in such an inconsistent manner.

Dave Anderson again mixed up the team selection, a recurring theme now the league title has been settled and everything is geared towards appearing in the FA Vase final. Lewis Gallifent was again in goal. From our game two days previous, Sam Flegg, Lewis Jackson, Jake Baxter and Michael Peacock returned as starters. Team management in discouraging match fatigue, keeping injuries to a minimum and not seeing referee coloured cards, was the priority again. It just about worked out. It was the statistical disappointment of failing to keep the goal tally rising, something that had consistently been achieved in competitive matches up to that point, being the main disappointment.

It did not make for exciting football. The only real moment of note in the first half was the game's only goal. Which arrived on the half hour. Had the infamous Dr Beeching of railway decimation in the 1960s fame been present then he would have had both goalkeepers withdrawn from service at the break for lack of customers. There was a bit more penalty area action in the second half, but not to any great degree.

Spectator verve was focussed more on howling at the referee than their players hardly managing to create scoring opportunities. The only really sustained period came as the end loomed when we tried to colour the game with one of our oft seen purple patches, but the moment faded after seven or eight minutes. The highlight at that time was a Sam Murphy volley that cleared the crossbar by a yard and a couple of other off target shots that punctuated a series of Chertsey Town corner kicks.

There might also have been a penalty award during an Andy Crossley thrust. The player went down under challenge, too easily for the referee's liking and a yellow for simulation was issued. Although well placed, the man with the whistle could be forgiven for not seeing the forearm administered on the other side of the entangled bodies, but that's the hustle and bustle of contact sport. All seeing fans behind the goal were not in such a philosophical mood at the time.

Time then did run out. Abbey's win confirmed their third place in the table and we got through without serious injuries or the devastation red cards to spoil someone's end of season jamboree at Wembley in mid May. All parties, therefore, came away more or less satisfied, even if the occasion failed to live up to the intensity that a KT15 v KT16 match might be expected to engender.

The Mighty Chertsey Town

By now the backlog of matches courtesy of the late winter weather and the FA Vase cup run had caught up with the team, playing 12 games in the month of April, averaging three games a week. It is remarkable that they didn't lose more games during the final run in than just this one and their success during this period is indicative of the strength and determination of the team and the astute use of the whole squad by Dave Anderson. Everyone had a role to play and, apart from a couple of uncharacteristic stumbles in the final run in, met the challenge when called upon.

Monday 22nd April – CC League   Horley Town 2 Chertsey Town 2

Although the grand total amounts to two dozen, nineteen regular names have featured overall on our team sheets in the nine Combined Counties League games played since winning their FA Vase semi-final tie. The away Bank Holiday trip to Horley Town presented no difference with juggling skills for manager Dave Anderson as his team ploughed through a particularly intense programme of six games over twelve days. This was the fifth in that sequence.

Countering fatigue and general battle weariness is a high feature for consideration as the Chertsey Town squad merry-go-round continued. One new name was added to the roster in Harry Healey, previously at Hillingdon Borough, who played with the number seven shirt. The morning game kicked off in bright sunshine but at a careful pace.

We almost camped out in Horley's half of the pitch for the first ten minutes but it was the home side that almost, and should have, taken the lead with James McGilligott firing wide from a tremendous position. Horley began to get a grip despite Sam Murphy heading wide. Then the host's Alex Barbary broke through and with only goalkeeper Lewis Gallifent in the way, contrived to lob the ball too high, consigning another gilt edged chance into the ether.

Alice Graysharp with Chris Gay

It could hardly be said that we were being besieged as those metaphorical green shoots of attacking options began to re-emerge. But in the meanwhile, yet another really good opportunity arose for the home side. A cross from the right was hooked away by Sam Flegg, just a foot or two from the goalmouth as a Claret shirt was about to pounce. Another nailed on chance was spurned by the home side when a forward somehow allowed the ball to pass through his two legs from a low cross when a tap home was all that was required.

They might well have been well behind in race to create chances, but we were still looking a half decent side. Evidence of frustration became apparent in attack as a desperate Jake Baxter shot from distance that was never going to find its mark was executed as the interval break loomed. The second half was almost a mirror image of the first except that goals did arrive. It was our turn to reflect on what might have happened.

It was the home side that secured the first. It came on 47 minutes from the penalty spot with Ryan Smith sweeping it away after a push when the ball had been hoiked in from the right. Too much pressure was put on the forward as he met, but knocked the ball over the bar. The scores were drawn level soon after with a swiftly taken Sam Murphy free kick that caught the Horley Town defence napping. However, Baxter was alive to the situation and drove forward with ball and smashed it past George Hyde.

The goal, and fresh young legs with Artie Tallboys coming on for Michael Peacock, on the hour, sparked us up and we began to look like the real thing. A Glenn Yala stinging strike hit the inside of the upright as we looked ever menacing. If we thought the earlier conceded penalty was a soft one then the same could be said for that sustained by Horley when Fred Hill was dragged down. It happened in the 65th minute which, with Baxter just about putting the ball away from the spot, put us into the lead.

A thunderous shot from Hill was touched onto the woodwork by Hyde that could have pulled us away enough to secure victory but instead, the home side came back eight minutes from time. On this occasion, a long throw placed the ball in front of goal. From a distance, it appeared a game of heading tennis then took place with the ball being successively knocked in the air. It was thus, not cleared. This situation only ended when Chad Goulter finished off the rally with the equaliser

Both sides had massive chances to race off into the distance. Both sides might moan about the penalty kicks. Neither could be rueful for having to share the spoils though on the day.

Fred Hill

Fred Hill, who was so close to a winner at Horley Town, was signed from Redhill in December 2018. Only just hitting his twenties now, he was with Corinthian Casuals in his younger days. While not featuring in the FA Vase Final squad, he played in left wing back or midfield positions in several league games during the latter part of the season and proved himself a versatile player, providing more depth to a squad still grinding out results in the closing weeks of the season.

Wednesday 24th April – CC League Guildford City 0 Chertsey Town 1

Part of the game with Chertsey Town of late has been to guess which players will be involved in any particular match. The visit to Godalming to play Guildford City was no exception, but even with the final games of the regular season nearing their end, this exchange failed to give a real clue as to what the Vase final squad might be.

Neither Sam Flegg, Sam Murphy, Jake Baxter, Dale Binns nor Lewis Driver were anywhere to be seen. Nick Jupp returned to goal after a two match absence. Keven Maclaren returned to his familiar number four shirt after missing the last five outings. Andy Crossley, Danny Bennell, Arlie Tallboys, Lewis Gallifent and Mason Welch-Turner made up an unlikely bench, but only the former got any play time when Lubo Guentchev was replaced midway through the second half.

The game took on a familiar pattern with the home side holding fast, even if most of the play was in their own territory. We had the best of the chances in the first half. Dave Taylor thought he had put us one up after just seven minutes with a far post header off a Guentchev free kick but it was ruled offside.

We came closer though, a dozen minutes later with a Harry Healy shot that found the far left hand post, but the ball flew away to safety. It was then the turn of the home side to have a goal disallowed for offside, much to the chagrin of the striker who received a yellow for his protestations.

The second half produced greater suggestion of a goal arriving, more likely from ourselves. A curling strike from full back Lewis Jackson was followed, on 56 minutes, with a special effort from Guentchev. He received the ball deep in the midfield and engineered enough space to let fly from outside the box. The ball sailed through the air, albeit like one with a following force nine gale. It then dipped into the net, giving goalkeeper Stuart Norman no chance.

Both John Pomroy and Glenn Yala attempted glancing headers that could have produced more danger for the home side than was the case. Crossley's introduction brought more right wing action and he was often successful in sending the ball over to the centre but, although it produced promise, the Guildford City defence were up to the job in protecting their own goal frame.

There was little danger at the end, apart from one raking run by Eli Ogunseye whose speed created menace all evening. He broke through to close range but the run and threat of an equaliser was eventually snuffed out. More likely success came from Yala with two stinging 18 yard shots, the second in follow up, that both visibly pained the wringing hands of Norman, but he kept his goal intact.

The game concluded with us still on the attack as we wound up our performance, not quite as a crescendo, but certainly with enthusiasm and ambition that belied the otherwise punishing schedule of matches having to be completed. A good one for the travelling fans that again boosted the attendance into three figures.

Saturday 27th April   Chertsey Town 1 Spelthorne Sports 3

The after-match presentation of the Combined Counties League championship cup was not tarnished by our first home defeat of the season against a very lively Spelthorne Sports. The visitors' energy and focus outdid us and, in taking three of the four good chances offered, enhanced their position in the table to sixth.

The grinding concentration of recent matches, combined with the prospect of the Vase final, probably had an effect on the side that seemed to be operating a little below their normal boiler pressure. It was not a half-hearted performance, but tentative passing and a feeling that physical challenges were not as decisive as usual resulted in the Chertsey scalpel not being so sharp.

Nothing can be taken away from the visitors. They came to do a job, and exercised their plan to near perfection, so were deserved of the points. For us though, the real prize was lifting the league trophy with at least ten points to spare. The last half dozen matches were more akin to enhanced friendly fixtures. Hats off to the greater squad though for seven bonus points have been collected since knowing the league title had been secured.

Alice Graysharp with Chris Gay

If Spelthorne Sports were given little opportunity to hit the net, then we were afforded even less. Our goal, when it did come late in the day, was from the penalty spot. Some bright moments were generated for the entertainment of the crowd, but not enough to create the sort of siege of oppositions' goals that have been a feature of our campaign.

Spelthorne gave an early warning when number five Graeme Edwards headed narrowly wide. But it was ten minutes later, on the quarter hour, when his colleague was more successful. Jake Flatman worked a good position virtually by himself through the middle, to let fly past Nick Jupp from 15 yards. If we thought that was a hiccup, then a reality check thudded down seven minutes later.

The reasoning was that another Flatman J goal was scored, this time with a headed effort following a cross from the left from brother Lewis who set it up by exploiting a breakaway moment with space to spare. It took the game to half time with Sports looking pretty.

The second period produced much the same fare as the first. Dave Anderson substitutions pepped up the pace of the game, with more resolution. However the effect was similar. Few chances were constructed. Passes at key moments were often misdirected or given the wrong weight. The margin of error was not great but it was enough for Spelthorne to shore up any of their own deficiencies.

Not much was pestering our defence either, but with us pressing up field, we were caught out again when addressing a very tight defensive cordon just at the moment Spelthorne launched a speedy left wing counter attack. The ball was crossed where only Jupp stood in the way, but he could not stop the inevitable five foot conclusion with Lewis Flatman tapping in the final nail in our casket, just after the hour.

Well, it was not quite the final act for we did pull one back to give the satisfaction of scoring a goal but even that was not from open play. Glen Yala came off the bench a while earlier and with fresh legs attempted to go round the right back, only to be dragged down in the process. Lubo Guentchev, more fresh legs off the bench teed up the spot kick and put it away with consummate ease.

Even though there was a dozen or so minutes remaining, there was never a strong threat that a point may be pulled out of the bag with one of our renown late rallies. Goalkeeper Henry Poole was required to save a creditable Lewis Driver strike, but the afternoon belonged to the visitors. That was until after the final whistle when a more substantive cheer was raised, with the championship cup, when captain Kevin Maclaren, as talisman for a hugely successful squad of players, took possession of the trophy.

Kevin Maclaren

I've saved the best till last. Kevin Maclaren is a huge reason behind Chertsey Town's extraordinary season. Some players' decisions to join Chertsey were influenced by his presence at Chertsey, a number had played alongside him before and his reputation in the non-league world went before him.

Kevin's hoisting high of the Combined Counties League championship cup was the realisation of the choice he made little over a year earlier to move from Kingstonian to Chertsey Town. "I joined Chertsey with about seven or eight games to go in the 2017-2018 season. I was playing for Kingstonian at the time and received a phone call from Dave Anderson. A mutual friend had told me Dave was in talks with Dave Rayner about taking over at Chertsey Town. I told our friend to tell Dave to ring me as I wanted to begin the step into management and Chertsey sounded like an ambitious club. The whole project excited me and after a couple of conversations with Dave he really impressed me too. I decided to help Dave towards the end of that season in what was a relegation battle. Probably the best move I ever made in football to be honest."

As captain, Kevin's influence on Chertsey's game has been massive. Unafraid to put in tackles when needed, organising, cajoling, encouraging his team, he was just the captain Chertsey needed to help bring the dream to fruition. He is aware of a reputation that he feels may be a little undeserved. "I think people can get the wrong impression of me when they see me play or see me around the football club. I always get told I look angry. I think I must just have a miserable face. I can be quite intense and serious on the pitch. But away from the pitch I'm very laid back, polite and have time for everyone."

Looking back over the year Kevin reflects, "We were brought in to do a job and we done it. I've now backed up what I sell myself as. I've captained a team throughout a remarkable season and nobody can ever take that away from me.

"I've played in many teams and with hundreds of players. Only a select group have the drive and attitude to win week in week out. Only a small percentage have the mental strength to deal with pressure and play in big games on a regular basis. Only the few have a cool head to pick the right pass or not get drawn out of position in critical situations during a game. There are many players who don't understand that performances or stylish football is irrelevant if you aren't winning. This bunch at Chertsey can win games however we need to. By playing pretty football or by playing 'ugly' football, by winning the game in the first half or by winning it with the last kick. We have lots of 'winners' at this club and it's important we stay together for as long as we can. Surround yourself with winners and you'll be successful.

"That's the overriding feeling I have about this season. Myself and Dave Anderson spoke regularly before and during the season. Dave's definitely a 'winner' by the way. We wanted to surround ourselves with like-minded people and it worked."

Tuesday 30th April – CC League   Chertsey Town 3 Abbey Rangers 1
Although this was our last Combined Counties League match of the season, and for a while at least, and ended on a controversial note, the evening was a testament to the year on year improving overall standards of the competition. The game was the Alwyns Lane derby with next door Abbey Rangers who have also excelled themselves with a third place in the table, their best ever position.

The controversy occurred in stoppage time whilst enjoying a one goal lead. Many thought there was a foul on an attacking Abbey player but play was allowed to continue. Players stopped, but not Jake Baxter. He was alone just inside his own half, and behind all out field defenders. On collecting the ball he advanced the required 50 yards and rounded goalkeeper Liam Stone to put the ball away with the opposition in the distance, still in high dudgeon.

There might have been a sniff of an equalising goal coming from the sought for free kick, but the odds would have been, as ever, with the defence so a Chertsey victory was still the more likely, especially as the final whistle blew moments later. It was a shame that the ending was fraught with negative emotion from one side on an otherwise open and positive evening.

Manager Dave Anderson again rested, in the genuine sense, players as his strict rotational system wound through. Dale Binns, Mason Welch-Turner, Sam Murphy and Nick Jupp were those missing at the start. It was not easy to work out the prime side as all players in the expanded squad work well together with a system.

An early scare came when Jack Wattis broke through but only found an upright instead of the back of the net. We tried to reply through Baxter off a Lubo Guentchev cross, but it was well saved by Stone. The ultimate defender did not do so well on the half hour though. A free kick, 30 yards out and to the left, saw Andy Crossley strike for goal. It looked likely to be a regulation save but the ball skimmed off the goalkeeper into the path of a grateful Lewis Driver.

Guentchev, soon after, fired wide when in A1 position and Baxter stung the hands of Stone with another rasper. It left us looking the better side at the break, but it has been a tradition, quickly built up in these exchanges, that a one goal advantage is never enough for comfort.

John Pomroy appeared off the bench as the second half progressed. One wonders if this might be his last competitive appearance at Alwyns Lane. He has been written out of the Curfews script before but has always bounced back, so who knows! It was a shame, therefore, that he did not actually score with one of his classic hooked shots from 35 yards, to the right. The ball flew just wide but almost caught out Stone.

But prior to this near magical moment, we had a double chance on the hour. Firstly Guentchev went close after he rounded Stone, but his stab at goal allowed a defender to cover. The same man was again denied after sliding in off a Baxter cross. Stone was on hand this time.

Elliot Frith forced a Lewis Gallifent fingertip save to clear the Chertsey bar on 74 minutes. It came close for the scores to be levelled but instead, we opened the gap further in the 83rd. It was another Abbey defensive error when the ball was sliced at whilst attempting a clearance. It opened up the way for Baxter to fire home from 15 yards.

The competitive edge of the game was far from finished as the gap was reduced within a minute back to the one goal after a superb 25-yard strike from Frith put heart back into a far from flagging Abbey Rangers. In fact they searched hard for an equaliser with Gallifent again employing fingers to divert high, another strong shot. A Ben Kersley header from a left wing cross also looked dangerous but flew wide.

But it was us as hosts who had the final say with the stoppage time success curtesy of the Baxter runaway goal. It signed off our championship winning season by increasing our lead at the top to a substantial, and far from just 'lucky,' thirteen points. It also came in tandem with the prospect of an FA Vase final and new pastures at a high level next season for fans to savour. Magic moments for Chertsey Town.

Postscript

A football club is like a body; some parts may be more vital to its basic function than others but, as I found out on breaking a bone in my hand recently, the body works a lot better if its component parts are all pulling together. An eye might not need the hand to function as an eye or the hand an ear to work as a hand but all are bound together for one common purpose. Thus a non-league football club cannot hope for success without a suitably talented and experienced football team and manager, an army of hardworking unpaid officials and volunteers, a band of loyal supporters and the means of underwriting the finances of the club.

Appendix 1 lists the club's officials for the 2018-2019 season. Their contribution and long service should not go unrecognised. An example is the Hon President, Chris Norman, who as the local Council Leader forty odd years ago wanted his commitment to the local community to reach beyond politics and has since then served as the club's President while juggling his civic duties until retirement, including becoming the Mayor of Runnymede in 2000. Steve Powers stepped up to Chairman from Vice-Chairman in 2001 and Sue Powers serves as Match Secretary.

The advent of Mark Turner as the Club's Commercial Manager has seen the transformation of the ground and of the club's commercial culture, his organisational skills exemplified by the highly successful long distance away trips. Then there's the financial backing and practical support from Dave Rayner which have in turn generated publicity for the club through newspaper and magazine articles about the season's realisation of his dream.

The service and dedication of the club's physio and his team deserve mention too. "Gary Anderson our physio," Kevin Maclaren says, "is someone I have great admiration for. I've got to know him on a personal level. He offers his services to the club and in the long run it costs him money! He also has plenty going on away from football and sometimes I ask him what he's been up to that day or this week and I'm astonished as to how busy he is. It must be mentally and physically tiring but he's never let us down and provides us with care that you couldn't find at many professional clubs. You don't get to manage Team GB for nothing and much like Dave Anderson he's really shown us his class this season." Michael Kinsella, whose ankle was broken in March, also has reason to laud the physio team. "In theory I was ruled out until September 2019 but I came back in time to train a week before Wembley and I got on the bench. A great achievement from myself to get back but I couldn't have done it without our superb medical team of Gary Anderson, Harry O'Driscoll and Jade Dorian."

Then there's Chris Gay, our Club Secretary of 40 years.

And Andy Pearson, the club's photographer, whose service began 25 years ago and whose first job as a committee member was to clean the dressing rooms after a match. Having done lots of odd jobs around the ground, especially in the close seasons, he ended up back as post-match cleaner, though not much fun in past years "after a loss on a dark, cold, wet and muddy winter evening match!" Like other committee members he helps out where he can, sometimes behind the bar and he administers the club web site www.chertseytownfc.co.uk.

For Andy, "this season has got to be the pinnacle highlight season for me as I have enjoyed the club league and FA Vase success particularly as club photographer travelling to some away matches and being asked by the local paper sports editor if I would be willing to let them use my pictures in the publications to save them sending up a photographer."

All those listed in Appendix 1 deserve medals too for their commitment to Chertsey Town football club. Read the names and acknowledge their dedication and relentless service that has contributed to the club we know today.

Among them also are the Rockhey family – mum Yvonne, dad Jack and daughter Rachel (also the Club's Treasurer to the end of the 2018-2019 season) who also serve at the turnstiles game after game, a regular commitment and also a financial responsibility. The Rockheys have run the gate for the last ten years, fans from nearly a decade before, Jack having been first introduced to Chertsey Town by Andy Pearson to help out with building work in 2000. Andy takes up the story. "Simon Harris and I undertook the task of repairing the ceiling in the female toilets at the tea bar end. We had clearly bitten off more than we could chew and struggled. It was then that I enlisted the help of a builder friend, Jack Rockhey, to advise us. Little did he know what he was letting himself in for at the time!"

Jack Rockhey praises the season's football as "very positive" and for Rachel it was "a good season football-wise," and having themselves put in much practical work over many past close seasons, they "got the reward last season for all the hard work over the years."

There are many other unsung, unlisted, heroes of the club whose dedication deserves recognition too along with other loyal supporters, their enthusiasm and vocal encouragement at matches acknowledged by the players as providing the 'extra man' in crucial matches. Supporters David and Trisha Payne, like Chris Gay, have been coming to Chertsey Town for over 60 years. David came as a teenager, while Trisha's father played for Chertsey Town when she was a child and brought her along to matches. Dave Smithies, living in Chertsey all his life, played for Chertsey Town in the early 1970s and still supports them from the terraces. Ian Payne lived in Chertsey in the 1980s and still comes despite having moved away; for him "the season for the club was as much for the town, it was unbelievable!" Pepe first came to know Chertsey Town through Dave Rayner in 1988; he played for various local non-league sides in his twenties, has played for Chertsey Town Veterans and was on the committee in the 1990s. For him the 2018-2019 season was "the best season I can remember, even when I was playing football." Pepe has a round trip of 55 miles to every home match, though not as far, he says, as another supporter who comes up from Bournemouth. Amongst other, more locally based supporters, is Barry Jones who moved to Chertsey in 2003 and became a regular this season – having seen Chertsey win 5-0 away to Redbridge he thought, "This could be going somewhere!" For him winning the league was the ultimate achievement as "the cream rises to the top whereas in a cup match anything can happen." Dave Smithies sums up Chertsey Town's season in one word. "Brilliant!"

Whether long serving members of the club, givers of finance and/or time and/or practical contribution, spasmodic returners or recent arrivals, whether players or backroom staff, youth team or the juniors lining the entrance of the teams for the semi-final second leg, all have played their part in creating the Chertsey Town Football Club that took the League and FA Vase by storm in the season 2018-2019.

From the Secretary's Quill

Chemistry is not only confined to the laboratory. It is alive and kicking at football clubs when every once in a while the elements combine in such a way to create something special. It could be said, and has been by some, that this occurred 25 years ago, but this season must surely fit into that category with even greater density.

You can have a well-respected manager, a well-respected coach, a talented set of players, on paper at the very least, and a hard-working club committee doing all the right things. However, that combination does not necessarily mean that the system is going to produce substantial success as a result. It has this time though.

Somehow, the combination has to gel into one entity to get the real result, and that is what I think we have at Alwyns Lane today. We are all cogs, engaging with each other at the club. Okay, some ratchets are bigger and less clogged with grease than others, but it only takes one bit of this matrix to fall off its spindle for all the clockwork to potentially fail.

Managers and coaches are key elements in setting up a happy, co-ordinated and effective dressing room. Equally, officers of the club also have a vital task to pro-actively contribute if the

Alice Graysharp with Chris Gay

service of the club is run efficiently with a motivated work force of volunteers. This mish-mash of parts has come together this past year to produce a truly momentous season.

I have been bumbling along with the club for quite some time, mainly through many unattractive campaigns of pain and misery. One of the key factors that got me through much of the bland times has been my family. It is not just my wife who, despite having scant interest in football, has constantly supported my efforts not just by giving succour or elbow room at home to allow the club to dominate that domestic scene. She has also given up hundreds of hours, mainly with kit washing and tea bar duties. I suppose over the eons, she has also spent hundreds of pounds in bits and pieces for the club, but who is counting.

My two children, having to take second place to the Curfews when young, have also given fantastic support with hundreds of hours given. Martin for his club shop in days of yore but now also with many hours of technical support, sometimes saving the day when a programme was in danger of not being produced. Daughter Susan too, has spent, I don't know how many hours, in the tea bar, mostly in the past but even now, she is still familiar with its interior.

Even my grandchildren are now being sucked into the workforce. Katie has also worked the tea bar at times and Ben set up CDs for match day broadcast and been on general gofer duties when required, as occurred last week.

It is therefore great pleasure that the pending final has presented the opportunity to say thank you for all their support over four decades. It means a lot to me, but I know that others can be said to be in a similar position so it is wonderful that the club has the opportunity to say thanks to those for past endeavours, as well as those giving more recent assistance,

Post Postscript

The drawing to a close of Chertsey Town's momentous league season is not complete without mention of the 2018-2019 Under 18s manager responsible for a future generation of Chertsey Town talent. John Waghorn's service of the club is also counted in decades. After moving to Chertsey in 1971, having started to attend Chertsey Town games he wanted to get involved in the local community through the club. "I have always been involved in youth work so when the opportunity came along to get involved with the youth team I jumped straight in and over the years I have made many friends."

Managing the youth team has had its moments. "At a youth game a few years ago I asked one of our committee members to lock the referees' changing rooms after the half time break, off he went and there we all were two teams ready for the second half wondering where the officials were and then suddenly a horrible thought crossed my mind and, yes, my nightmare had come true, he had managed to lock all three officials in the changing rooms, so off I went to secure their release, apologising profusely!"

Reviewing the current Under 18s Team's season, John says, "With the season coming to an end, Chertsey Town Youth finished a very respectable eighth in the Central Division of the Isthmian Youth League; a very tough competition when you consider the quality of the opposition we encounter week in week out. Also to note is the fact that eight of the ten sides run as academies. Therefore, it is a great achievement to beat them or run them close. It just shows what can be done with hard work and application.

"The highlight of the season for me was when we played away at Carshalton Athletic who were then top of the league, but we defeated them 2-1 on their 4G pitch in a battling performance. The low point was when we were thumped 5-0 Kingstonian in a game where, if it could go wrong, it did. We all have those moments in life so we just have to 'move on,' dust ourselves down and start all over again.

"Sometimes you just have to put your hand up and admit that you were beaten by a better side, which was the case with the Met Police who also beat us 5-0, but they are a very good side as their growing collection of silverware will confirm. It was a great finale to the end of the season when we managed to win four of our last league games only losing out to the league and cup champions, so things are looking good for next season as we hope to retain a lot of the younger lads and complement them with some new summer signings.

"We have at times struggled to find the net on a regular basis but this all changed when Gus Naya scored a hat-trick when we defeated Tooting & Mitcham 5-4 earlier this month. Then in our last game of the season, we defeated Chipstead 4-2 with some cracking strikes from Aaron Petch, Josh Daily and two from Arlie Talboys.

"If we look back over the season, I think we could consider it a success. Two lads from the previous term started the season with the first team and moved on to gain first team experience at other clubs before they will hopefully return one day. Gus Naya, Patrick Marshall and Arlie Talboys have all played cameo roles for the first team this season so overall I think we can consider it 'job done'."

The job was not entirely done for the first team who were now preparing for the most momentous day in the lives of Chertsey Town FC's footballers, officials and supporters…

SPRING 2019

Dave Taylor at Northwich Victoria away (beyond their number 5) sending the ball goalward…..

….and into the net!

The Mighty Chertsey Town

1-1 after 90 minutes away and 120 at home (plus stoppage)….

it all came down to penalties and….

Chertsey putting away four penalties to Northwich Victoria's three, going to Wembley is now dependent on Sam Murphy's spot kick….

Alice Graysharp with Chris Gay

We're going to Wemberlee!

The Mighty Chertsey Town

Sam Flegg

Lewis Driver

Fred Hill (above) and Kevin Maclaren (below)

Lubomir Guentchev (yellow number 7)
scores at Hayes away

Champions away at Hayes AFC

Lifting the Combined Counties Premier
League Champions Cup

19TH MAY 2019

In the 2018-2019 season 638 teams entered the FA Vase competition, 296 teams entered the FA Trophy competition and 92 league clubs entered the League Cup competition. Between those three competitions alone (the FA Cup is not included here as the same teams enter the FA Cup competition), assuming average squads of 18–20 players, that's between 18,468 and 20,520 footballers dreaming of Wembley. As Mason Welch-Turner points out, "Not too many people can say they've played at Wembley in a final broadcast live on BT Sport and it makes it even sweeter doing it with a team my dad has played for and a team I played for when I was 14."

The Chertsey Town players got there in style, beating the bookies' favourites, West Auckland, on the way, and holding their nerve to execute five perfect penalties which, together with Nick Jupp's crucial save, won the semi-final against a legendary non-league club. Behind the team was a group of Club officials of whom Kevin Maclaren says, "I'm delighted for people like Dave Rayner, Mark Turner, Chris Gay, Sue and Steve Powers. Chertsey Town is 'their' club. They probably never expected to see their team play at Wembley, and probably never expected to win the FA Vase. To be part of a group of players who made that a reality for them means everything to me."

"A huge mention," adds Andy Crossley, "needs to go to the fans and the people behind the scenes at the club that have supported us all over the country this season which has been unbelievable!!"

Michael Peacock also reflects on the importance of the FA Vase to the supporters and the wider community. "The Vase has affected the town itself, attendances have increased and brought more interest in the club again, but what this all meant to the people around the club, one fan said to me he'd been waiting 60 years for this to happen to Chertsey and this makes you realise what we were able to do for the fans."

Fans were now making their plans to attend the final. In Dublin my sister booked another day return trip. Other fans were planning longer journeys. When Chertsey Town reached the semi-final Andrew Robins in Thailand "told the wife I may need to pop over to the UK for a couple of days if we make it to the final which we did."

The ultimate in one-upmanship, though, came from Mick Bashford who travelled 53,000kms from Brisbane, Australia. Mick played as a junior for Chertsey Town in the 1970s and in the late 1990s he served on the Chertsey Town Committee. "I used to prepare the half time refreshments and boardroom platters for after the game with a fantastic group of ladies. Often checked up on the progress from my new home in Australia, but when I heard the news we were in the semi-finals of the FA Vase, I started thinking… if we actually do… I'm going!!!!!" Mick and Andrew even managed to meet up at the Golden Grove on the Friday before the Final.

There was also a contingent of supporters from Northern Ireland. Dave Anderson recalls, "When I was a lad in Belfast me and my mates loved playing a game we called Wembley and some of them came over to watch the final."

Posters appeared all over Chertsey urging "Come and support your local team at Wembley Stadium." Hodders Estate Agents acquired four tickets for which they ran a competition where the competitors just had to visit Hodders' website and enter their name, number and email address, and Hodders gave the winners scarves and flags as well.

Dave Rayner is "pleased what the club going to Wembley did for the town of Chertsey itself. There was a great feeling in the town and people would come up to me in the car park and thank me for what I'd done to help get Chertsey there." Mark Turner sees the Club's success as having "put the town itself back on the map. I've had lot of thanks and appreciation from people coming up to me in the town."

The club continued to treat the players like royalty and a hotel was organised for the night before the final which further fostered the team spirit engendered in the away trips of the later rounds. Dave Rayner recalls, "A great memory of the trip to Wembley was at the hotel the evening before the final when a video was played comprising the good wishes of lots of people culminating in one from David Beckham."

For Dave Rayner, "Going to Wembley in the FA Vase Final was the fulfilment of a dream I'd had since I was aged around 9-10. The school I went to supplied ballboys and I was one of them. My dream was to play at Wembley and I'd have pursued that if it wasn't for a bad leg break which ended my footballing hopes. So the only way to get to Wembley was to take a non-league club there."

Eight and a half months after Chertsey Town's first victory in the FA Vase competition, they walked onto the hallowed turf. "Stepping out on the pitch at Wembley in front of 6,000 of your friends and family and the loyal Chertsey Town fans," says Jake Baxter, "was amazing." Mark Turner agrees. "The crowd at Wembley was brilliant. It was amazing to step out and see all the Chertsey Town fans."

While Chertsey Town were the bookies' favourites in the Final, their opponents were not to be underestimated and Cray Valley PM (the PM standing for Paper Mills), which had just achieved promotion from the Southern Counties East League (Step 5) to the Isthmian League South East (Step 4), went ahead after passing play on their left wing ended with a shot from Gavin Tomlin on 36 minutes.

Undaunted, Chertsey pressed forward and were rewarded three minutes later when Sam Flegg's header from Lubomir Guentchev's corner hit the post, the ball rebounded straight back and was volleyed in by Sam Flegg from close range.

Cray Valley were the more lively of the two teams but as the 90 minutes crept close Chertsey Town's discipline and solidity in defence held them at bay, although in the last minute of normal time Cray Valley's defender Anthony Edgar burst through seemingly certain to score but saw his shot hit the bar, a huge let off for Chertsey Town and perhaps the moment that turned the game. For in extra time Lubomir Guentchev was brought down, adjudged by the referee to be just inside Cray Valley's penalty area and Jake Baxter stepped up and scored the resultant penalty. Chertsey Town were now in the ascendancy and late on a flowing one-two with Guentchev saw Quincy Rowe unleash a curling shot from the edge of the penalty area which beat the 'keeper and took the score to an irretrievable 3-1. So much were Chertsey Town now in the ascendancy that the score could have been bettered had not the Cray Valley 'keeper saved a late Guentchev shot onto the post and then tipped over a last Guentchev effort.

John Pomroy has a special reason to thank Quincy Rowe for his goal. As Dave Anderson explains, "The hardest part of the job was the big decision to leave players out. Andy Crossley, Lewis Jackson and Dave Taylor for example all deserved to be in the Vase Final starting line-up. I would always pull players one on one who weren't starting in big games before we went in the dressing room. But in the final I pulled the ones who would have been worried to tell them the FA were allowing seven subs and they were definitely on the bench." Three of these subs were allowed on up to the end of normal time and by the end of the 90 minutes all three had all been used. The FA rule allowed for one more sub during extra time but, says Dave Anderson, "I decided that at 2-1 unless anything else happened I'd keep things as they were. Then Quincy Rowe (who I nearly dropped for the final for being late!) scored and I got to bring John Pomroy on which was perfect as he's such a legend at Chertsey and he had stayed on when so many others had left in the previous season, he deserved to be playing at Wembley."

For Chertsey Town fans seeing Chertsey Town at 3-1 up and John Pomroy running onto the pitch for the closing minutes of the game the day really couldn't get any better. Bearing in mind his selfless aside to Andy Crossley the previous evening, it was the very least reward the Chertsey Town legend deserved. Pomroy says, "All the time I have spent at the club, eighteen years on and off, these trophies were the first I've won for the club. Winning the double means everything to me, to walk up the steps at Wembley and lift the cup in front of my family and so many Chertsey supporters."

Winning the Double, culminating in the Wembley win, was an experience enhanced for the three players who scored the goals. Sam Flegg feels he has "achieved something so special, especially having scored in the final." Though ultimately, "the biggest thing for me was having so many of my friends and family in stands at Wembley – that made it extra special." Jake Baxter agrees that "to score a goal at Wembley and get the win there's never been a feeling like it. I was just really happy to have scored. My dad was there watching, he has always put so much time and effort into me growing up, playing football, or just being a dad so it was nice for him to be able to see me score at Wembley as I felt I gave him something a little back." The FA Vase Final was for Jake "the best day in my football career and which is never likely to be beaten."

For Quincy Rowe "the best thing about the season was winning the FA Vase and scoring a goal. The Vase Final day was the best day of my life."

Also in the winning team at Wembley was Dale Binns. For him, winning the Double is "the perfect way to end the career and chance got my kids and the family to have some lasting memories of me playing, and to finish with a win at Wembley is more than a dream come true."

Nick Jupp "had all my family at Wembley and my friends had hired a coach there. So seeing all of them in the crowd at Wembley was something special."

The importance of family is echoed by Kevin Maclaren. "To give my friends and family a great day out at Wembley is something I'm very proud of. The response from them all has been incredible. I'm now a couple of my friends' sons' new hero! It's fantastic."

And for one of the players, "Wembley was a better day for me than my wedding!"

The euphoric feeling is echoed by other players, even those who didn't play in the FA Vase Final. Lewis Gallifent finds winning the Double "amazing, I'm only 18 and I could retire now and be happy about my career." Michael Kinsella, whose season was so cruelly brought to a premature end, sees winning the Double as "massive for the town of Chertsey. The club is on the map again and I can take this season with me for the rest of my life. Incredible!"

For Michael Peacock, "Winning the league and the FA Vase this season has been amazing, it has been the best achievement of my career. To be able to compete on both accounts takes a serious level of attitude, commitment and obviously ability. The character of team is unbelievable, there are times we looked down and out but managed to claw a result out. We also had a real tough run to get to the final of the Vase, teams with real pedigree in the tournament and all away from home, so to go to these teams, put a game plan into place and come out winners is incredible.

"The FA Vase is really special achievement, there are hundreds and hundreds of professional players who never get to Wembley, not only did we get to play there but to win and walk up the famous steps and pick up the trophy was just an amazing feeling which made me forget how tired I was, I was just buzzing, something I will never forget."

Lubomir Guentchev reflects on the importance of team spirit in the side's achievements. "Hand on my heart, I can easily say, I have not been in a team, squad, family like Chertsey. In the dressing room, there has not been one single fight amongst us. There are no cliques. When one is down, we all help him get back up. This was the key to our success this season." And for Lubo, "Reaching Wembley is something else. A dream come true… huge understatement! Winning there is unmatched. No words can describe the feeling. I was more excited to see everyone that was a part of Chertsey smiling and living this moment with the club.

"When it all settled down later that night, I left the bar heading back home to meet up with my family that were at the game, and an elderly man stopped me and said, 'You know, I've waited 60-plus years to see something like this in our town.' Still brings goosebumps everytime. At the end of the day, that's what it's about. Memories. We sure did write one down in the history books. The Curfews!"

Lifting the Vase was Dave Anderson's last act as Chertsey Town's manager. "Immediately after the Final and before I had to talk to the media I told the team I was retiring as I wanted to tell them first. The players took the news good humouredly as they'd been expecting it." On telling the team he was retiring, one of the players said "Thank f**k for that!" "It cracked me and the dressing room up," says Dave, "and was a measure of the great bond the whole group shared."

Dave Anderson reflects that, "if AFC Wimbledon's meteoric rise through the leagues while I was manager there was pure Hollywood, then what Chertsey Town achieved was a fairy tale come true. You couldn't make it up. And I'm still dwelling on the memories of the season. If I'd stayed in management I'd have had to get my head down right away preparing for next season but now I can get on with just enjoying the success."

Supporters too found the season's success rounded off with a Wembley victory as amongst the best times of their lives. For Steve Powers it was "spectacularly unbelievable. Winning the league and winning at Wembley was like being in a dream, like watching *Match of the Day* but with your friends and family in the crowd!" Simon Harris, who first came as a thirteen year old "eating chips in the stand" and on the committee since 1998, "never believed I'd end up sitting in posh seats in Wembley. It still hasn't sunk in and I have to look at the banner, flags and so on to realise it really did take place." In David Payne's 60 years of following Chertsey Town, "it was something the club thought they'd never do. The crowd at Wembley was fantastic. The club has been in the doldrums over the years and that made being at Wembley so great."

For longer distance traveller Andrew Robins, "the whole trip was well worth it, really chuffed to see Chertsey get on the map." He had seen Manchester United win the FA Cup twice at Wembley, "but Chertsey Town's winning the Vase topped both of those." And Mick Bashford, all the way from Australia, "wouldn't have missed it for the world."

Meanwhile, Andy Pearson, dressing room post-match cleaner for Chertsey Town, couldn't resist the opportunity being treated as a VIP at Wembley provided. "Of course I had to indulge in a photo of myself emulating cleaning out the England dressing room at Wembley after our match as well as others with the cup and sitting in the England Manager's dug out seat. It really was a fantastic day."

The day was round off with a celebration at the Crown in Chertsey afterwards. The players were cheered by crowds of supporters as they disembarked the team coach. At the presentation that followed the awards were as follows

Committee member of the year – Mark Turner
Young player of the year – Lewis Gallifent
Players' player of the year – Michael Peacock
Committee's player of the year – Nick Jupp
Supporters' player of the year – Jake Baxter
Golden boot (for highest scorer) – Jake Baxter
Special award for services to the club – John Pomroy.

Kevin Maclaren was announced as the new Chertsey Town first team manager.

St Peter's Church flew the Union Flag for the week following the Final in celebration of Chertsey Town's achievement.

To round off a remarkable season the Chertsey Town team and officials took part in the Black Cherry Fair Parade through the streets of Chertsey on 13th July 2019, proudly displaying the two cups in an open top bus and later signing team photographs for eager fans at their Black Cherry Fair stand.

19TH MAY 2019

We're on our way to Wembley….

We're there!

The Mighty Chertsey Town

Sam Flegg (immediate left of number 7)
scores Chertsey Town's first goal

Celebrating Chertsey's first goal

Chertsey attacking...

The Mighty Chertsey Town

and defending…

Alice Graysharp with Chris Gay

Jake Baxter takes the penalty and…

scores Chertsey's second goal

Celebrate!

The Mighty Chertsey Town

A chance late on

Who put the ball in the Valley net…

…Quincy, Quincy

John Pomroy is a Legend!

The Mighty Chertsey Town

Pommers and Kevin Maclaren hold the
Vase aloft…and Dave Anderson too

The celebrations continue at the Crown Hotel, Chertsey

The Mighty Chertsey Town

Black Cherry Fair

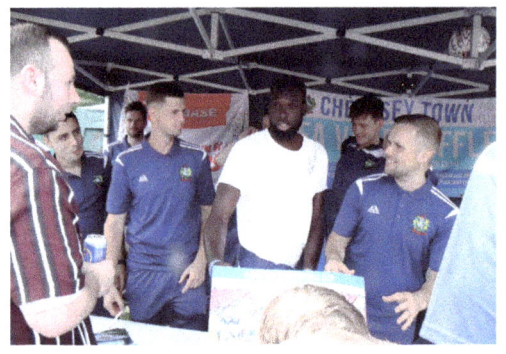

APPENDIX 1

Chertsey Town FC Membership 2018-2019
(with year joined the committee)

PRESIDENT – C. Norman (1991)
CHAIRMAN – S Powers (1997)
VICE CHAIRMEN – J Waghorn (1989) & A Hyman (2004)
SECRETARY – C Gay (1974)
TREASURER – Miss R Rockhey (2005)
COMMITTEE – A Pearson (1997), S Harris (1998), J Rockhey (2002), Mrs S Powers (2009), Mrs S Hyman (2009), E Jeffrey (1992-1997 then 2010), Mrs Y Rockhey (2009), A Kimble (2013), K Davies (2016), H Naya (2018), S Vassell (2018), D Rayner (1988–1996, then 2018), R Allen (2018), M Turner (2018), Mrs S Harris (2011-2015, then 2018).

Chertsey Town FC Honours

FA Challenge Vase Winners 2019, Quarter Finalists 1985 & 1992
Surrey Junior Cup Winners 1897
Surrey Junior League Winners 1920
Surrey Senior League Champions 1959, 1961 & 1962
Surrey Senior League Challenge Cup Winners 1961 & 1962
Spartan League Runners Up 1975
Spartan League Cup Runners Up 1975
Combined Counties League Champions 2019, Runners Up 1986, 2010 & 2011

Combined Counties League Cup Winners 1986
Surrey Senior Cup Finalists 1986
Isthmian League Division Three Runners Up 1992
Isthmian League Cup & Charity Cup Winners 1994
Isthmian Associate Members Trophy Winners 1994
Isthmian League Division Two Runners Up 1994
Southern Combination Cup Winners 1998-99
Staines Charity Hospital Cup Winners 1964

APPENDIX 2

Combined Counties Premier Division
Final League Table 2018/2019

	P	W	D	L	F	A	Gd	Pts
Chertsey Town	38	28	7	3	97	41	56	91
Sutton Common Rovers	38	23	9	6	85	48	37	78
Abbey Rangers	38	21	4	13	64	60	4	67
Southall (-1)	38	19	8	11	68	47	21	64
Raynes Park Vale	38	17	9	12	47	48	-1	60
Spelthorne Sports	38	17	7	14	69	47	22	58
Guildford City	38	17	4	17	62	66	-4	55
Banstead Athletic (-1)	38	14	13	11	57	48	9	54
Badshot Lea	38	14	8	16	52	69	-17	50
Horley Town (-1)	38	14	8	16	59	67	-8	49
Knaphill	38	15	4	19	53	71	-18	49
Redhill	38	13	8	17	62	66	-4	47
Colliers Wood United	38	13	7	18	64	72	-8	46
Cobham	38	12	9	17	62	66	4	45
Hanworth Villa	38	13	6	19	54	64	-10	45
Camberley Town (-3)	38	13	8	17	63	65	-2	44
CB Hounslow United (-3)	38	13	6	19	59	69	-10	42
Balham	38	11	7	20	55	69	-14	40
AFC Hayes	38	11	7	20	51	68	-17	40
Walton & Hersham	38	8	9	21	61	93	-32	33

APPENDIX 3

First Team Results, Scorers and Appearances 2018-2019
Curfews first team results, scorers & appearances

Opponents	Date	Ven	Comp	Score	Scorers	Att	1	2	3	4	5	6	7	8	9	10	11	Substitutes
Hanwell Town	Sat 14 July	A	Frly	2 1	Harbridge Binns		Bennett	Newman	Coleman	MacLarenK	Peacock	Kinsella	Morgan	Taylor	Pomroy	Jackson	Binns	MacLarenC Ferguson Smith Harbridge Baptiste Yala Colombian
Chalfont St Peter	Tue 17	A	Frly	0 2				Baptiste	Bennell	MacLarenK	MacLarenC	Kinsella	Jackson	Peacock	Pomroy	Smith	Morgan	Colombian Ferguson Harbridge
Ascot United	Sat 21	A	Frly	1 0	Harbridge		Bennett	Baptiste	Bennell	MacLarenK	MacLarenC	Kinsella	Jackson	Peacock	Harbridge	Pomroy	Morgan	Colombian Ferguson Smith
Egham Town	Thur 26	H	Frly	0 0														
Harrow Borough	Sat 28	H	Frly	2 2	Ferguson Smith													
Camberley Town	Sat 4 Aug	A	League	2 1	Binns Murphy	102	Jupp	Jackson	W/Turner	MacLarenK	Kinsella	Bennett	Murphy	Taylor	Smith	Morgan	Binns	MacLarenC A/Peters Pomroy Gallifent Crossley
Hanworth Villa	Tue 7	H	League	1 0	Binns	117	Jupp	Jackson	W/Turner	MacLarenK	Peacock	Bennett	Crossley	Taylor	Pomroy	Murphy	Binns	Smith Driver MacLarenC A/Peters Gallifent
Arundel	Sat 11	A	FA Cup	1 4	Smith	75	Jupp	Jackson	W/Turner	MacLarenK	Peacock	Bennett	Murphy	Taylor	Smith	Pomroy	Crossley	MacLarenC A/Peters Gallifent Ferguson Harbridge Kinsella
Raynes Park Vale	Sat 18	H	League	4 1	Jackson Peacock Smith Crossley	74	Jupp	Jackson	W/Turner	MacLarenK	Peacock	Bennett	Murphy	Taylor	Driver	Pomroy	Crossley	MacLarenC A/Peters Gallifent Smith Kinsella
Southall	Sat 25	A	League	1 0	Taylor	85	Gallifent	Jackson	W/Turner	MacLarenK	Peacock	Kinsella	Harbridge	Taylor	Driver	Murphy	Crossley	MacLarenC Smith Pomroy Ferguson Yala
Knaphill	Tue 28	A	League	4 0	Smith Murphy MacLarenC	101	Jupp	Jackson	W/Turner	MacLarenK	Peacock	Kinsella	Smith	Taylor	Driver	Murphy	Crossley	MacLarenC Pomroy Ferguson Gallifent Bennell
Woodley United	Sat 1 Sept	H	FA Vase 1Q	2 2	Pomroy 2 Smith Guentchev	92	Jupp	Jackson	W/Turner	Taylor	Kinsella	Bennett	Crossley	Ferguson	Smith	Pomroy	Guentchev	Binns Gallifent Harbridge
Hurley Town	Sat 8	H	League	3 1	Guentchev Binns Crossley	85	Gallifent	Jackson	Cousins	MacLarenK	Peacock	Kinsella	Guentchev	Taylor	Driver	Crossley	Binns	Murphy Smith Pomroy MacLarenC Bennett
Tadley Calleva	Sat 15	A	FA Vase 2Q	1 0	Guentchev	148	Jupp	Jackson	Cousins	MacLarenK	Peacock	Kinsella	Guentchev	Murphy	Pomroy	Crossley	Binns	Smith MacLarenC Gallifent Taylor Ferguson
Hurley Town	Tue 18	A	League Cup	1 0	Pomroy aet	64	Gallifent	Jackson	A/Peters	Taylor	Peacock	Kinsella	Harbridge	MacLarenC	Smith	Ferguson	Guentchev	Pomroy Bennett MacLarenC Crossley Talboys
Cobham	Sat 22	H	League	2 1	Murphy Guentchev	85	Jupp	Jackson	Cousins	MacLarenK	Peacock	Kinsella	Guentchev	Taylor	Pomroy	Murphy	Binns	Smith MacLarenC Ferguson Gallifent W/Turner
Sutton Common Rovers	Sat 29	A	League	1 1	Crossley	70	Jupp	Jackson	W/Turner	MacLarenK	Peacock	Kinsella	Crossley	Taylor	Baxter	MacLarenC	Binns	Smith Ferguson Gallifent Pomroy Bennell
Colliers Wood United	Sat 6 Oct	H	League	3 0	Baxter 2 Crossley	62	Jupp	Jackson	W/Turner	MacLarenK	Kinsella	Bennett	Guentchev	MacLarenC	Baxter	Murphy	Crossley	Gallifent Pomroy Binns Taylor Ernesto

Flackwell Heath	Sat 13	H	FA Vase 1	6 1	167	Baxter 3 Ernesto Guentchev 2	Jackson	Gallifent	Jackson	W/Turner	MacLarenK	Peacock	Kinsella	Guentchev	MacLarenC	Baxter	Murphy	Crossley	Pomroy Binns Ernesto Bennell Bennett
Redhill	Tue 16	A	League	4 1	70	Baxter 2 Binns Guentchev	Jupp	Kinsella	W/Turner	MacLarenC	Peacock	Bennell	Guentchev	Murphy	Baxter	Crossley	Binns	Gallifent Pomroy Ernesto Davis Jackson
Walton & Hersham	Sat 20	A	League	1 4	170	Baxter 3	Jupp	Jackson	W/Turner	Taylor	Peacock	Bennell	Guentchev	Murphy	Baxter	Crossley	Binns	Pomroy Ernesto Davis Jackson Gallifent
AFC Hayes	Sat 27	H	League	3 1	105	Baxter 3	Jupp	Jackson	W/Turner	Kinsella	Peacock	Bennell	Guentchev	Davis	Baxter	Crossley	Binns	Pomroy Ernesto Gallifent Taylor MaclarenC
Horndean	Sat 3 Nov	H	FA Vase 2	2 0	169	Binns Peacock	Jupp	Jackson	W/Turner	Kinsella	Peacock	Bennell	Guentchev	Taylor	Baxter	Crossley	Binns	Pomroy Ernesto Gallifent Bennell Davis
Spelthorne Sports	Sat 10	A	League	2 1	80	Guentchev Taylor	Jupp	Jackson	W/Turner	Kinsella	Peacock	MacLarenK	Guentchev	Taylor	Pomroy	Crossley	Binns	Ernesto Gallifent Bennell Davis McClarenC
British Airways	Tue 13	H	League Cup	3 2	61	Binns Davis	Gallifent	Talboys	W/Turner	MacLarenK	Naya	Bennell	Ernesto	Marshall	Pomroy	Davis	Binns	Jackson Kinsella Guentchev Bennett McClarenC
Banstead Athletic	Sat 17	H	League	3 3	115	Baxter Becka Kinsella	Jupp	Jackson	W/Turner	Taylor	Kinsella	Bennell	Guentchev	MacLarenC	Baxter	Crossley	Binns	Ernesto Gallifent Davis Pomroy Becka
Walton & Hersham	Tue 20	A	Surrey Snr Cp	2 2	75	Guentchev Pomroy (5-3 pens)	Gallifent	Talboys	W/Turner	Becka	Kinsella	Bennell	Davis	Jackson	Pomroy	Ernesto	Guentchev	Taylor Jupp Naya Marshall Crossley
Guildford City	Sat 24	H	League	2 2	108	Baxter 2	Jupp	Jackson	W/Turner	Taylor	Peacock	Kinsella	Guentchev	Murphy	Baxter	Crossley	Davis	Ernesto Gallifent Pomroy MaclarenC Binns
Redbridge	Sat 8 Dec	A	FA Vase 3	5 0	68	Murphy 3 Baxter Binns	Jupp	Jackson	W/Turner	MacLarenK	Peacock	Kinsella	Guentchev	Murphy	Baxter	Crossley	Binns	Gallifent Pomroy MaclarenC Taylor Bennell
Walton & Hersham	Sat 15	H	League	5 0	91	Murphy 2 Baxter MacLarenC	Gallifent	Jackson	W/Turner	MacLarenK	Kinsella	Rowe	Guentchev	Murphy	Baxter	Crossley	Binns	MacLarenC Taylor Bennell Hill Bennett
Balham	Sat 22	A	League	2 1	84	Baxter 2	Gallifent	Jackson	W/Turner	MacLarenK	Peacock	Rowe	Crossley	Taylor	Baxter	Murphy	Binns	MacLarenC Davis Hill Pomroy Kinsella
Knaphill	Sat 29	H	League	3 1	148	Baxter 4 Binns	Jupp	Jackson	W/Turner	MacLarenK	Peacock	Kinsella	Crossley	Taylor	Baxter	Murphy	Binns	MacLarenC Davis Hill Pomroy Gallifent
AFC St Austell	Sat 5 Jan	H	FA Vase 4	3 0	501	Baxter 3 Murphy Guentchev	Jupp	Jackson	W/Turner	MacLarenK	Peacock	Rowe	Guentchev	Murphy	Baxter	Crossley	Binns	Davis Pomroy Gallifent Kinsella Taylor
Sutton United	Tue 8	H	Surrey Snr Cp	1 0	161	Taylor	Gallifent	Davis	Bennell	Jackson	Peacock	Kinsella	Guentchev	Taylor	Pomroy	MaclarenC	Binns	Crossley Baxter Rowe MaclarenK
Hanworth Villa	Sat 12	A	League	2 0	95	Baxter Murphy	Jupp	Jackson	W/Turner	Taylor	Kinsella	Rowe	Guentchev	Crossley	Baxter	Murphy	Binns	Davis Pomroy Gallifent MickyersC Hill
Abbey Rangers	Tue 15	H	League Cup	1 2	172	Baxter	Gallifent	Davis	Bennell	MacLarenC	Kinsella	Rowe	Guentchev	Taylor	Pomroy	Murphy	Crossley	Baxter Naya Matsell Green Bennett
Camberley Town	Sat 19	H	League	1 0	130	Baxter	Jupp	Davis	W/Turner	MacLarenK	Kinsella	Rowe	Guentchev	Murphy	Baxter	Crossley	Hill	Pomroy Gallifent Taylor Binns MaclarenK
Raynes Park Vale	Sat 26	A	League	2 2	52	Binns Pomroy	Jupp	Jackson	W/Turner	Taylor	Kinsella	Rowe	Guentchev	MaclarenC	Baxter	Murphy	Binns	Crossley Pomroy Gallifent Hill Davis
Badshot Lea	Tue 5 Feb	H	League	2 1	71	Binns Baxter	Jupp	Flegg	W/Turner	MacLarenK	Peacock	Rowe	Guentchev	Murphy	Baxter	Crossley	Binns	Pomroy Gallifent Davis Taylor Kinsella
Irlam	Sat 9	A	FA Vase 5	2 0	449	Guentchev Baxter	Jupp	Flegg	W/Turner	MacLarenK	Peacock	Rowe	Guentchev	Murphy	Baxter	Crossley	Binns	Pomroy Gallifent Davis Taylor Kinsella

			Surrey Snr Cp															
Walton Casuals	Tue 12	A	League	1-3	Taylor	138	Gaillient	Jackson	Bennell	MacLarenK	Pomroy	Kinsella	Guentchev	Taylor	Bates	Davis	Crossley	Naiva Mansell Green Bennett Peacock W/Turner
Sutton Common Rovers	Sat 16	H	League	2-2	Taylor 2	238	Jupp	Flegg	W/Turner	MacLarenK	Peacock	Rowe	Guentchev	Taylor	Baxter	Murphy	Crossley	Gaillient Davis Kinsella Driver
West Auckland Town	Sat 23	A	FA Vase Q/F	2-0	Binns Rowe	730	Jupp	Jackson	W/Turner	MacLarenK	Peacock	Rowe	Guentchev	Taylor	Baxter	Murphy	Binns	Gaillient Kinsella Driver Pomroy Bennell
Redhill	Tue 26	H	League	2-1	Taylor Driver	137	Jupp	Jackson	W/Turner	MacLarenK	Kinsella	Rowe	Guentchev	Taylor	Baxter	Murphy	Crossley	Gaillient Driver Pomroy Hill MacLarenC
Balham	Sat 2 Mar	H	League	4-1	Guentchev 2 Crossley Baxter	142	Jupp	Jackson	W/Turner	MacLarenK	Kinsella	Rowe	Guentchev	Taylor	Baxter	Driver	Crossley	Gaillient Pomroy Murphy Binns Bennell
CB Hounslow United	Tue 5	A	League	4-0	Baxter 3 Bennell	95	Jupp	Jackson	Hill	MacLarenK	Bennell	Rowe	Guentchev	Murphy	Baxter	Driver	Binns	Gaillient Pomroy W/Turner Taylor
Northwich Victoria	Sat 23	A	FA Vase S/F 1	1-1	Taylor	1288	Jupp	Flegg	W/Turner	MacLarenK	Peacock	Rowe	Guentchev	Taylor	Baxter	Murphy	Binns	Gaillient Pomroy Bennell Driver Jackson
Northwich Victoria	Sat 30	H	FA Vase S/F 2	0-0	aet won 5-3 on pens	1847	Jupp	Flegg	W/Turner	MacLarenK	Peacock	Rowe	Guentchev	Driver	Baxter	Murphy	Binns	Gaillient Pomroy Crossley Jackson Taylor
Colliers Wood United	Tues 2 Apl	A	League	3-3	Baxter OG McCluskey	81	Gaillient	Jackson	Hill	MacLarenK	Flegg	Bennell	YalaG	Taylor	Baxter	McCluskey	Crossley	Hope Murphy Baxter Rowe Jupp
Banstead Athletic	Thur 4	A	League	2-1	Driver Guentchev	103	Jupp	Jackson	W/Turner	MacLarenK	Peacock	Bennell	Guentchev	Taylor	Baxter	Driver	Murphy	Gaillient Pomroy Hill Binns YalaG
Badshot Lea	Sat 6	A	League	3-0	MacLarenK Baxter Flegg	112	Jupp	Jackson	Hill	MacLarenK	Peacock	Flegg	Guentchev	Murphy	Driver	McCluskey	Baxter	Gaillient Pomroy Binns YalaG W/Turner
Cobham	Tue 9	A	League	2-0	Jupp	110	Jupp	YalaG	W/Turner	MacLarenK	Flegg	Bennell	Guentchev	Taylor	Baxter	Driver	Crossley	Gaillient Pomroy Hill Binns Jackson
Southall	Tue 13	H	League	5-1	Driver 3 Pomroy 2	283	Jupp	Jackson	W/Turner	Taylor	Flegg	Rowe	Guentchev	Murphy	Baxter	Driver	Binns	Gaillient Pomroy Hill Bennell Crossley
AFC Hayes	Tues 16	A	League	3-1	Guentchev Jackman Crossley	147	Jupp	Jackson	Bennell	Taylor	Peacock	Rowe	Guentchev	YalaG	Baxter	Driver	Hill	Gaillient Pomroy Crossley W/Turner Flegg
CB Hounslow United	Thu 18	H	League	4-2	Binns Crossley Pomroy Jackson	170	Gaillient	Artie	W/Turner	Taylor	Rowe	Bennell	Crossley	Binns	Pomroy	Murphy	Hill	Guentchev YalaG Jackson Peacock Bennett
Abbey Rangers	Sat 20	A	League	0-1		178	Gaillient	Flegg	W/Turner	Jackson	Peacock	Rowe	Guentchev	Murphy	Baxter	Crossley	Hill	YalaG Bennett Talboys Bennell Pomroy
Horley Town	Mon 22	A	League	2-2	Baxter 2	75	Gaillient	Flegg	W/Turner	Taylor	Peacock	Bennell	Healy	Murphy	Baxter	YalaG	Hill	Guentchev Jackson Bennett Pomroy Talboys
Guildford City	Wed 24	A	League	1-0	Guentchev	117	Jupp	Jackson	Hill	MacLarenK	Peacock	Rowe	Guentchev	Taylor	Pomroy	Healy	YalaG	Gaillient Crossley W/Turner Bennell Talboys
Spelthorne Sports	Sat 27	H	League	1-3	Guentchev	193	Jupp	Flegg	W/Turner	MacLarenK	Peacock	Bennell	Murphy	Taylor	Baxter	Driver	Binns	Gaillient Crossley Pomroy Guentchev YalaG
Abbey Rangers	Tue 30	H	League	3-1	Baxter 2 Driver	187	Gaillient	Flegg	Hill	MacLarenK	Peacock	Rowe	Guentchev	YalaG	Baxter	Driver	Crossley	Jupp Bennett Pomroy Talboys W/Turner
Cray Valley PM	Sun 19 May	W	FA Vase F	3-1	Flegg Baxter Rowe	9896	Jupp	Flegg	W/Turner	MacLarenK	Peacock	Rowe	Guentchev	Murphy	Baxter	Driver	Binns	Gaillient Crossley Pomroy Bennell Taylor Kinsella Jackson

ACKNOWLEDGEMENTS

In bringing together the various threads with which this book is woven I am indebted to many people for their help, information and advice (any error or omission in the narrative is wholly mine!), including (in no particular order)

The Football Association (for its kind permission to reproduce extracts from the FA Vase Final Programme)

Chertsey Town FC players

Dave Anderson

Chertsey Town FC officials especially Dave Rayner, Mark Turner, Chris Gay, John Waghorn and Andy Pearson

Chertsey Town supporters

My supportive and proof-reader husband

The Clink Street publishing team

Alice Graysharp
August 2019

www.ingramcontent.com/pod-product-compliance
Lightning Source LLC
Chambersburg PA
CBHW070532090426
42735CB00013B/2958